POOR FROGGIE!

IF HE HAD ONLY

LISTENED!

THE POWERFUL DELUSION

Eric Boomer

ISBN 978-1-63630-195-2 (Paperback)
ISBN 978-1-63630-196-9 (Digital)

Covenant Books, Inc.
11661 Hwy 707
Murrells Inlet, SC 29576
www.covenantbooks.com

INTRODUCTION

Frogs live in the water!

Water is not a threat to them!

It is my intention to show how old and how slow and how backward I am in today's technological age. At least that is what some (most) will think of the message that will be contained in this book. I'm going to approach a subject that will offend even the most casual reader. Why? Well, because the subject matter has to do with the common everyday life, with things that are necessary to living, and things that can't be put aside or replaced with other avenues. As a matter of fact, the very instrument that I'm using to write this dissertation will be the subject matter. Yes, you have guessed correctly—the computer! And if push came to shove, it isn't the instrument but rather the plan behind the instrument that I desire with God's help to uncover.

During the uncovering process, it will be revealed that we are truly not as far removed from our first parents, Adam and Eve, as we would think. We have been given the command that we should not eat from the tree of the knowledge of good and evil...and yet there is that consistent crunching of forbidden fruit sounded every single day. As we look at the fruit, we see that it is good for food and it's hard to get a job without it. The fruit is pleasing to the eye. There are so many things that look so good. We know that the same fruit is desirable for gaining wisdom. What could ever be so wise as to have all the wisdom of the world bound within the center of the fruit?

Now we know that eating the fruit caused a lot of trouble for those who ate from the forbidden tree, and it caused a lot of trouble for the rest mankind. Think of it this way: if I'm wrong, you will have proven that I'm old and technologically challenged; but if I'm right and this message is from God...there will be *hell* to pay!

THE POWERFUL DELUSION

How many times have you been tricked into believing something only to find out that you had been deceived and now your money is gone? That you were made to look the fool? That you went to meet them and they weren't there? That they promised us fewer taxes? Most of us can recall the time and the place. We can even picture the face of the person and how much we were angered or disappointed by them. It even seems that we find others that resemble the guilty party and have a dislike for them immediately. We don't like being deceived!

Second Thessalonians 2:11 tells of something that people refuse to talk about with a sincere heart and as if their very lives depended on it. The subject matter is important to you and me and holds the future of mankind in the hands of the loving Master of the universe. It's his warning to the very people that he loves...and yet few take him seriously.

> For this reason God sends them a powerful
> delusion so that they will believe the lie. (2 Thess.
> 2:11 NIV)

First of all, are we so gullible that someone could deceive *us*? First reflections: no way could we be deceived! We have superior intellect and a grasp on what is going on around us! Sure we do! That's why we fall for the latest deal, and it turns out to be a bad deal. Or perhaps we place our trust in our brilliant savings plan only to see the financial institution close or the stock fall out of sight. Maybe it's failure to see why the coworker looks so good only to find out after divorce they're human just like our mate was. Oh, friend, we are gullible in every way and can be deceived by our wretched hearts into believing just about anything! That pleases *me!*

It's with this in mind that I begin this first chapter and just a little peek into the unknown to ask the question, *What is the powerful delusion?* Is there something or someone that is playing the con game with people so that the kingdom of the Antichrist can be set up? (Read all of chapter 2 of 2 Thessalonians.) The second question I would ask is, *Why are people so prone to move toward the lie?*

Our first inclination is to think that Satan is the one that will send the delusion because he is the father of lies. When we look at how stupid Satan has acted throughout history, we have to believe that he is not capable of coming up with such a plan. After all, he is the one that lived in the presence of God and had been given position, provision, and power, and chose to leave it all behind. He found that he was in a no-win situation opposing his own Creator, and the end result was his own demise. How smart is that?

Paul states that God sent them the delusion and used Satan to do his bidding. It wasn't the first time he had done that, and it wouldn't be the last. God wanted Job to have a greater relationship with him, so he allowed Satan to tempt Job. It was painful, but it worked! God wanted to save mankind from their sins, so he allowed Satan to nail Jesus to the cross after beating him almost to death. It was painful, but it worked. The bad part of this scenario is that Satan can and will tempt. The good part is that he will always cause the will of God to be done. He is permitted to go only so far. The bad part is that he is permitted to appeal to the desires of men's hearts which are deceitful and wicked. The good part is that if man will trust in the promises of God, man will *win* every time, and the deception will not work.

Let's begin our journey with poor little Froggie. Maybe it will help us to feel what is happening to the human race in today's world. Maybe it will help someone to realize what is happening to *them.* The little green fella has a lot to say to a lost and dying world and a church that can't seem to get its feet back under itself.

Froggie came into this world just like any other ol' frog, with hundreds of black, slimy brothers and sisters and not a leg to stand on. Froggie was born into a great ocean of liquid that was way bigger than anything he could imagine. It's a good thing that he was waterproof, or he might have drowned. His life wasn't what you would call exciting or anything like that. Nevertheless, he enjoyed swimming around and playing with all the rest of the kids. Like any other self-respecting tadpole (that's what they call kid frogs), he began to grow legs and arms, and with that, there seemed to form an element of pride in how fast he could zoom through the water. His brothers and sisters turned green with envy at his accomplishments. Well, I guess they were all turning green. It was just part of the process of growing up and becoming a "frog." True to his name, known far and wide, he began to be a little more "froggie" from time to time. So much so that the others gave him that name.

"Froggie, you're going to get in trouble someday, and you're going to lose all the good things God has given you."

But Froggie wouldn't listen because he was *king* of his domain. He knew what he was doing. Froggie could handle anything!

The very beginning of Froggie's demise was his pride in the fact that it was *his* domain, and *he* knew what *he* was doing, and *he* could handle it! With all our programs and seminars and titles and accomplishments, one would think we knew and had taken lessons from Froggie (or he from us). First John 2:16 speaks directly to that pride, and we ignore the wisdom that God has given us.

> For everything in the world—the cravings
> of the sinful man, the boasting of what he "has
> and does"—comes not from the Father but from
> the world.

The church world isn't exempt from the outcome of boasting who has the largest church or who received the most members or who brought in the most money or who has the biggest building. Accomplishment means a lot to this day and age. We seem to be success driven. We did this, and we did that, and so we would like to share with you this information so that you could "succeed" too! I want you to know that our desires change from spiritual to earthly, and that alone prepares our minds to be deceived. As we walk away from dependency on God, he will allow something to replace that void in our heart. Something that *we depend on*, something that *we spend our time with*. Why? Because he wants us to know that everything other than the God of the universe will fail us. He has to send us the delusion so the god we have come to love will be shown for what it is—false and dead!

Now as we move toward Froggie's demise, let's keep in mind that the game that is being played is for keeps. After this life is over, there will be no return to try and do it right the next time. The judgment will be final, and we won't be able to say that it wasn't our fault and that we had been deceived. Zechariah 10:2 tells of idols speaking deceit. In the *King James Version*, the Word says that they speak vanity. Both are equally correct because pride and deceit go together just like a hand and an arm. One is not complete without the other.

Froggie's biggest problem was his *big* mouth bragging about what he owned and what he could accomplish. Let's not forget the fact that frogs don't *own* anything.

Now, folks, we didn't evolve from a frog, but we are not that far removed from the slimy little creatures that we should think that we own anything either! If we owned it, we could take it with us when we die. If it were ours for keeps, others could not take it away from us.

In other words, we have what we have because God has given it to us to care for (Gen. 1:26). We are no better than Froggie and should not think that we are. God owns the cattle on a thousand hills and the wealth in every mine. But, dear one, he also owns the hills and *everything* else. Period...end of sentence! He doesn't die; we do! He doesn't leave anything behind; we do! Everything that God has created, he could create again...and again...and again. The dusty ole earth that we live on has no appeal to him. God does not have to brag about what he owns so that he can impress some highfalutin bigwig. Let's look and see how Froggie's doing in his big pond that he lives in.

Living in big ponds presents a lot of problems to little frogs: fish that swoosh out of nowhere and eat you; men that sneak along the bank and gig you (spear you with a three pronged pitch fork); wild animals that wait in the bushes and snatch you up and eat you before you know what is happening.

Well, now, Froggie had survived them all. His reputation had preceded him where ever he went. He only croaked when he wanted to, not when others decided it was his time "to go." By this time, the pond was full of frogettes and little froggies that looked just like him. It seemed that even the fish talked about him with sort of a... type of reverence. He was the "bull" frog of the pond. It's odd that one with such high-esteem would begin to forget where he had come from. It's odd that Froggie had all that he needed to be happy, and yet...his waterlogged brain would look for more—more land to conquer and possess, loftier words to be spoken to describe who the "frogster" was.

I know that the question has formed in your mind on how I could state that the computer has any part of the great deception that will be sent to the earth so the Antichrist's kingdom can be set up. Your question tells me that you have forgotten that this book isn't about the tool but rather the plan to *use the tool* for our demise. You seem so smart but have such a hard time staying focused on the necessary. You would rather go to a debtor's hell than see what is happening to our world. You can't seem to see past today and your own little bitty plan and what could possibly help your agenda, your likes and dislikes, your desire to prosper—just like Froggie.

Maybe if we took a little time and looked at why this age doesn't want to talk about the obvious, it would help to understand what is taking place.

What Froggie Doesn't Know Will Hurt Him!

Millions of people from around the world are taking the time and using the energy to fall before the god of this age, and they are losing contact with the living God of the universe. There are five excuses they are using today to condone their misuse of time, their broken relationships, and their idolatry. You don't have to listen to me, but it may be beneficial to your well-being if you would. Examine these five areas:

1. *You're archaic without the everyday/all-day use of the computer.*

In today's age, only those who are old and antiquated are against the use of the computer on a regular basis. Well, that does make sense... Well, doesn't it? Their mind doesn't function fast enough to keep up with how to use it, let alone keep up with the changes that are made monthly—almost daily. Every time you turn around, the stuff you bought yesterday is outdated. The barb comes in when the geniuses who have all the new stuff make fun of the slowpokes who haven't bought the new stuff, and millions are made with everyone trying to keep up.

Dear friend, we find that the desire to not get "left behind" creates a sense of dependence. It's more than technology; it's the fact that the now generation is afraid of getting older, and in fact, they are afraid of dying. To stay alive is to stay connected with the times!

Why, you will be able to stay connected to the younger generation, and heaven knows that we are losing contact with them!

> Froggie had heard the rumors goin' round the rumor mill. People takin' pond frogs into the big city and makin' 'em pets. Given 'em a safe place to live and all, food every single day, and no stinkin' fish to hafta worry 'bout. *"Utopia, that's what it was,"* they was sayin'.
>
> Then ol' King Frog heard 'bout the place that actually took applications so that lowly little froggies could help everyone have a better life. It was someplace called an instututee or somepun like that. They wanted to test your stamina and see what you were made of. Well, that fit right up Froggie's ego alley. No one had stamina like he did. He could swim further, jump higher, and go faster than anyone. His pride wondered what it would be like to show the world what he could do. He'd probably get a medal or somethin'. Maybe a palace of his own so people could know that he wasn't too old and that fer sure he wasn't dead yet and that *he was king of the pond!*

Pride is such a destructive weapon in the hands of the enemy. It caused Satan's downfall, and he knows that it will cause mankind's downfall. If only they will fall for the Great Delusion, their minds will fall for anything. They won't know that they are being led astray.

2. *The computer is so useful that one would wonder how we ever got along without it.*

These and comments like this come across my pathway all the time. Everything is made so much easier now that we have the computer. Very few take the time to consider the losses that take place because of the convenience that the computer world gives to us. Let's face it: so many tasks are made easier because of this valuable tool. But as long as we're taking a good look, let us look closely at the end result of making things "easier." You know that it is said, "Good hard work never hurt anybody." But there is the thought that if all things are made easier, the child gets spoiled, and he becomes very self-engrained. Before you know it, that child is demanding that all things serve him so he can "enjoy" life. That, my friend, is called *sin*. And though sin causes enjoyment for the moment, its wages are death. After all this time, the computer is now needed, and reality says that without it we would be lost. It is too bad that the disciples didn't have the computer. It would have made their job so much "easier" when it came to starting the church back then. Instead of meeting in Jerusalem on the day of Pentecost, they could have just sent an e-mail. Maybe that would have *netted* ten thousand souls for Christ instead of a mere three thousand. The coverage would have been so much greater and...

What do you think, Froggie? You got any insight into the need?

You know the saying "The grass is greener on the other side of the fence"? Well, Froggie knew that saying well. Sure enough, it came back to him that the pond had too many weeds... too little space...smelled too moldy...too many fish...not enough recognition. You know, ya have to see the negative before ya can see the positive. Besides, with all the progress that was takin' place, the pond would be swallowed in no time. Modernization seemed to be the only choice a frog could make—especially a frog of Froggie's standing. Just think of what was offered! No need to hunt for food anymore! Freshwater all the time! Ya didn't have to fight for survival anymore! How had he lived in this stinky ol' pond all these years? How could he have put up with the way God had intended it to be for poor little

froggies? This new world that was being offered
is so much more *useful!*

Isn't it amazing? You're still trying to defend that little bitty idol
to justify why you sit before it day after day. You still don't realize that
I am not talking about the tool but the plan behind the tool. And if
you can't make the transition in your mind, the "inner-net" may capture your heart forever. You'll have to renounce someone, and it will
probably be the one that you spend the least amount of time with.

Really! You see, dear friend, when we renounce something
or someone, it won't happen overnight. First, we become dissatisfied, and then we begin to see the "other" in light of the advantage
that will be coming into our lives. Do you think for a minute that
someone has an affair because they want to destroy their home, ruin
their children's lives, or make what little sanity they have fly out the
window? They have that affair because they become dissatisfied and
then see someone that would bring advantage and pleasure into their
lives. It's slow, it's deliberate, and it's gripping. It doesn't let go until
the destruction has taken place. Let me tell you: *the plan* that will
take many to a debtor's hell is using the computer to bring us into
captivity…forever.

3.   *Using the computer saves us so much time that
     it gives advantage to our daily lives.*

I had a pastor friend who showed me into his study one day.
His church was a mini-mega church, and he was the type of person
that went on to be someone. Nice guy, gifted, and all that. As we
entered his domain, I was impressed by the décor. I was impressed
by the order and the many books that lined the shelves. I was even
impressed by the passion which seemed evident in his voice as he
showed me around. I was saddened when we went straight to the
computer and he began to show me how much time was saved by
the ability of the computer to pull up words from different verses
in the Bible that could then be slipped into sermon notes. He then
had time to do other things to "grow his church." He didn't mention

prayer time or Bible study, just the time he had saved. Yes, you're right. I am being unfair about his ability to grow a church. He did have a lot of gifting. Yes, he sure seemed to be getting the job done.

This thought comes to mind: Has the wonder of the computer caused us to lose the wonder of who God is and what God is capable of doing? Folks, it has taken a long "time" to reach this advanced age of technology. God created the universe and all that is in it in one week. Man strives to win people to the church and boasts about winning five hundred people over a ten-year period of time; it took one sermon from Peter and God won three thousand.

We could look closely and see that someone is trying to convince us that the computer can actually get things done faster and more efficiently than God can. It's odd, isn't it? We will wait on the computer to respond and tell us good news, and yet…we can't wait on God to tell what would be the most efficient way to get his work done. On one hand, we get an instant response that may gratify our impatient nature. On the other hand, we know that his ways are higher and greater, and yet in our hurry to get things done, we zoom into and past our prayer time and forget that God knows and desires to get us to slow down so that we can hear and listen to his voice. That's odd, isn't it?

We have worn ourselves out trying to handle it. We put things up on the screen, but we lose the anointing. We send out so many e-mails inviting people to our church that we lose the personal "time" spent with those we are trying to win. Why did the beginning church win so many and get so established—without the computer? We say and act like technology has given us the edge, and yet our stress level grows daily. Our deadlines seem to fall short, and we don't meet our goals. Why? I thought we were freeing ourselves to have more "time." Could it possibly be that we are being taken captive and our minds seduced to believe the lie and worship the created thing rather than the Creator?

Froggie had been on land so much that he almost felt at home. He seemed to stay close enough to the water's edge so that in one great leap he could land into the pond and safety. Some of his more unfortunate frog buddies had been captured and sent away, some to become "frog legs" in a frying pan and some to the institute or the place of higher learning. Froggie was too smart to be fooled. He liked his legs attached to his body, and he liked to think that he was the smartest frog around, and yet…one little trip to actually see where the smarter frogs went couldn't possibly hurt, could it? Pride will take even a genius to points beyond where he wants to go!

Well, the day was set, and the bags were packed, and the map was drawn. Froggie had exercised for weeks trying to build up his endurance. Yes, Mom and Pop Frog had tried to tell him not to go. But listen, they were so old that they had lost all their sense of adventure. They lived in their tiny little pond and lived in fear of what could happen. It was true that they had weathered many storms and escaped death more times than one could count. But…let's get real! Their minds weren't as sharp as they had once been. Even they would be amazed when Froggie came back with stories of grandeur, vision, and promise.

This will help all frogs in every pond!

Why, time-saving devices might be found so that Mom and Pop could live longer—maybe forever! Just because this brave soul would venture past the limits of his little domain! What a great frog to be so brave!

It seems that so many are trying to save time that they are missing the fact we are but a breeze that blows by in such a short time and then goes on into eternity. We're the flowers of the field that spring up and then fade away as we head for our eternal home. Who is going to get us there? The computer? Or God? One will save us time, and one will save us for eternity.

4. *Without it, you can do nothing.*

Oh, I'm right on this point. In today's age, you can do little without the computer. If I go to the store...yep! I have to use the computer. If I use my cell phone...if I get into my car, if...I do my banking...if I want send in my report...if I want something for a cheaper price...if I want to look up information...if I want to reach my friend overseas (now)...if I want to charge something...if I want to buy and sell... Wait just a cotton-pickin' minute! I've bought things, and I didn't have to use the computer. Folks, if I have to say it a thousand times, it's not the tool; it's the plan. We are headed toward a time that will drag us to where we don't want to go.

Someone is taking us to the place where our dependency will be placed on a tool and not the God who can save our souls. When we begin to trust the tool and those who craft and shape it for our convenience, the unthinkable will happen. Someone will step to the forefront and claim that without this tool we cannot buy or sell. If you have any type of thought process, you will admit that this is the direction that we are going. We are moving rapidly toward a cashless society. Well, ask yourself, how are we going to buy and sell? We are moving toward being numbered. They know more about you than you can remember. Traced and retraced, you're in the system. Your new car has a tracking device so that they know where you are and probably where you've been. You cannot rent a car or reserve a motel without a credit card. They have ads on television that tell you that people that use cash just slow the process up. They are old and antiquated. Online banking is not only the *in* thing; in some cases, it is the *required* thing. We are being primed for the takeover if we don't conform. The problem is that our minds are being shaped to conform. We can do anything without the computer. And because you still are being close-minded, let me quote from *the Plan* (God's Word) as to where the plan, not the tool, is taking us.

He also forced everyone, small and great, rich and poor, free and slave, to receive a mark on his right hand or on his forehead, so that no one could buy or sell unless he had the mark, which is the name of the beast or the number of his name. (Rev. 13:16–17)

Who of you has been forced to do or put up with stuff that pertained to the computer? I went to Wal-Mart the other day, and the lines were so long, and the line to the self-check was so short… No one forced me to use it, but convenience demanded that I do something that I didn't want to do. There are many other things that push us toward accepting something that we would not want to do in the future. Please use your brain, even if it is just for a minute. Here is the outcome to the matter.

A third angel followed and said in a loud voice: "If anyone worships the beast and his image and receives his mark on the forehead or on the hand, he, too, will drink of the wine of God's fury, which has been poured full strength into the cup of his wrath. He will be tormented with burning sulfur in the presence of the holy angels and of the lamb. And the smoke of their torment rises forever and ever. There is no rest day and night for those who worship the beast and his image, or for anyone who receives the mark of his name." (Rev. 14:9–11)

Chips in cars, chips in pets, stolen credit cards, stolen identity, chips in people! It is going to be so easy to number and identify and organize this generation because of the seduction of the mind and the fact that without it you can do nothing.

Froggie hopped on over the hill in search of the place of higher learning. True to form, his little following came with him. "Where we going, Froggie?" "What's going to happen to us, Froggie?" "Is it going to be fun, Froggie?" On and on went the questions. But then again, who cares when it comes to pleasing your black-spotted heart? They made him feel special, and rightly so because he, of course, was king of the pond. He ruled his domain. He called the shots, and at this moment of time, everything was goin' his way!

Good fortune was just about to pay off. The "following" was in awe when they came over the hill. Ponds were everywhere. Cool, clean water, fences to keep the predators out, food on plat-ters just sitting around…all to the pleasure of a gazillion other frogs that seemed to be having the time of their lives. Froggie just knew that he had made the right choice and his courage was going to make his "pond" proud.

Wasn't he amazed when the whole group was invited to join with the other frogs at some of the outer ponds! It seemed that they knew that his group was coming and they seemed to know how important Froggie was. Why, a fellow could really get used to this! As a matter of fact, after a few days, it became hard to remember the old pond. It was hard to remember old friends. It was hard to remember how things used to be. Mom and Pop sure were wrong about the outside world and technology. That's funny! I can hardly remember what Mom and Pop looked like. Oh well, I have found a new way of life, and I just don't think I could do without it!

So you see, folks, we are not as far removed from Froggie as one would think. We've moved into this technological age, and it's so great we just don't think we can live without it. In fact, we are coming to the place in our minds that we think strange thoughts. We are letting pride in, and we think we are "someone" because our "thinking" has advanced us so much farther than our forefathers. You might think that we have advanced past the Creator…the Savior… the King. It seems like the smarter we get, the dumber we become. Oh, now look what I've done. I have gone off and offended you because you were so proud of what we have become! We ask God for revival in our land, but we fail to humble ourselves. That was Froggie's downfall. That will be our downfall if we're not careful.

5. *This delusion is grasping everyone's allegiance.*

In today's age, people are looking for answers to some pretty tough questions. So instead of teaching math, we give our kids calculators. Instead of teaching them how to spell, we teach them how to abbreviate so they can text faster. We give them spell-check (thank God for spell-check). Instead of teaching them to be financially responsible, we give them plastic. Instead of teaching them to be able to communicate and participate with others, we teach them to go into a fantasy world on the Internet or perhaps Facebook where they can say anything they want. All these things and many more are products of the computer age, and we are going to receive the wages of what we are sowing. People are losing their ability to communicate—with God and with each other. You bet, they are saying words, but the heart-to-heart is being lost, and we are moved from feeling to feeling. What *on earth* makes me feel good?

One of the first things that makes me feel good is to feel part of the group. No one wants to stand alone or be rejected. I know how the saying goes, "I want to be different," but it's always "just like them." We fit into groups, and the computer age is an all-inclusive age. Grandmas and grandpas begin to text and e-mail so they will fit into their grandchildren's lives because they don't want to lose them. It's too bad that the grandchildren are not desiring to be like grandma and grandpa!

And though more and more people are moving toward becoming ingrained in the computer age, even the holdouts are having trouble because of the peer pressure (society-imposed pressure). And just like the proverbial fishing net that gathers the fish in, the Internet is sucking more and more people into its grasp than ever before. Not the tool—the plan using the tool.

> After weeks and weeks, there was Froggie sittin' on top of the world! What he was at the old pond, he was that much more at these new ponds. Everyone looked up to him as if he was the most important frog in the world. He was asked to speak at frog conventions. Others sought him out for advice. Still others asked if they could just sit around and watch him swim. This sure put him at the top of his game! He didn't realize that he was the leader and didn't have a clue where he was leading the others. You see, those inside the gate, those that had plans for those outside the gate, they were using Froggie to draw the others into their plans.

The plan is using the wealthy, the greatest athletes, the most knowledgeable, those in authority, the stars who are idolized, and those who rule to lead the people into what seems beneficial and what seems right. The plan is using these star-studded people to lead those who would not go unless they had someone they trusted and looked up to show them the "way."

People are taught to gamble because someone taught them that the numbers racket was okay. Now they call it the lottery. People were taught to have an affair because the favorite star showed them that it's permissible. They know how to cheat on their taxes because those in governmental positions cheated on theirs. They learned that it's all right to be greedy because those superathletes demanded exorbitant amounts of money to do something they loved to do as a kid. I could go on to prove my point, but if you're honest with yourself, you already know what I mean and that what I say is true. What you don't realize is that the tree of the knowledge of good and evil (what you would call the computer world) is teaching people to find Internet pornography right alongside their most-needed item. Those geniuses teach how beneficial it is and say that it is good. You say, "Show restraint"; I say, "Fish that are *netted* are swept away because of indifference and lack of knowledge." The plan has captured them; and they are being taken to the fish market to be gutted, chopped up, and given as food for the buzzards. Why do you think that one of the major downfalls in the pastoral world is Internet pornography? Take the leader down, and the house falls apart.

Pride Comes before the "Water" Fall!

Sure enough, Froggie was finally invited into the recesses of the gates that introduced him to the inner sanctuary. The place where anybody that was anybody went—could we say—as a promotion. Finally real recognition was setting in. It didn't matter that there were many others that were chosen. What mattered is that he, "King Frog of Podunk Pond," was getting his chance to make his mark on the world.

Oh my, it was a little frightening when what used to be the enemy came so close. Humans had always done harm to the frog population. But Froggie got the "feeling" that these humongous manifestations of mankind were different. They seemed so kind and so "gentle"!

Satan knows that if he told the world that he was going to plunge mankind into his clutches and into utter chaos, he would lose the majority of the people. He also knows that he must appeal to the heart of mankind instead of creating a plan that would be offensive to their own desires. What is also known is the fact that the light is standing in the way of darkness. The salt of the earth must be removed. The truth has to be replaced by the lie.

If the church is the problem that stands in the way of the plan working, a diversion must be created. Humans fall for created things more quickly than anything else. They are prone to idolatry whether in the church or out of the church. Like Aaron, like mankind, "Give us something we can *see* so we may worship God," and out popped the golden calf. Aaron was great at that point. The people wanted... so I gave them.

> Let us purify ourselves from everything that
> contaminates body and spirit, perfecting holiness
> out of reverence for God. (2 Cor. 7:1)

I'm going to attempt to give you five points that contaminate body and spirit. If you're still mad at me for thinking that some are so dull that they don't know what is happening, please get over it. What is being revealed will save your life.

The computer stops childlike faith.

I've examined childlike faith many times. First of all, Jesus said that we had to be like a child when coming to God the Father. They don't seem to ask for all the answers. They just take for granted that the parent (God) knows all the answers, and he will answer all the questions. He will supply all the needs. He will give all the directions, etc.

Secondly, he said that without faith, we cannot please God. Well, folks, when you have all the answers within fingertip reach, why would you have to trust someone that you can see? Google this or that, and the answer will pop up sooner or later. Within this mentality is the thought that God is too slow, that God doesn't come up with the answer I wanted, that God seems to be off in some foreign country and is not concerned with my problems. Most of all, faith in the unseen is replaced with the seen. A direct deviation from what God had intended for mankind. Sort of like "Trust me on this one. Don't eat the fruit." But faith that God is right gives way to sight. "But it looks so good, and I'll bet that it's good for food, and finally, it will give us the knowledge to see things like you do." All these things were true; but so was the wisdom that came with the command: when you eat of the tree of the knowledge of good and evil, your spirit will die to the relationship we had together. Did it happen? Was Adam separated from the Father? If we would only realize that anything that stops childlike faith causes death—to our relationship with the Father.

> Froggie just seemed to be a little foggie. Why was he trusting in the seen more than trusting in what his Father whom he couldn't see had told him? Why was he feeling so comfortable with those who he had known to be his enemy? Why did he feel like he was being led into some impending doom? Why did he feel as if he was losing his "kingship"?

The computer stops prayer.

I know. You think I have flipped my lid! Prayer goes on just like it always has. No, it does not. If we look closely, we will see that more and more time is spent on the computer, whether it is a phone computer, a laptop, or the one that sits on your desk. Less time is spent in deep soul-searching prayer that talks to God and then stays long enough to listen to what he has to say. God does still speak to his children, ya know. God still enjoys the time-consuming presence of his children, ya know. God still wants to talk to us about all sorts of stuff over and above what we need today...ya know?

Pastoring for thirty years has taught me several things about people. The average person can sustain praying for around five minutes. By that time, they have prayed everything that is known to their personal little world, and they seem to run out of important things to say. Many of these same dear folks either have never heard God talk to them and don't expect that to change, or they are in too much of a hurry to listen.

Picture this for just a minute. Seven ministers are standing in a hotel overlooking Jerusalem, the great city of God. Somehow, a conversation starts to play out with the idea that men cannot hear the voice of God anymore. In fact, yours truly becomes the topic of conversation. Having claimed that God has told me this and that during revivals about the needs of the church and various people, the discussion becomes quite intense, and six out of the seven adamantly stated that God does not speak to people in ways that men may say they have heard from God. He may be understood through the written word and through our voice as a minister but never because he has spoken to us personally. Wow! Do you know how many verses contradict this by saying you can hear God's voice?

The watchman opens the gate for him and the sheep know his voice. (John 10:3)

I have other sheep that are not of this sheep pen. I must bring them also. They too will listen to my voice. (John 10:16)

Whether you turn to the right or the left, your ears will hear a voice behind you, saying, "this is the way; walk in it." (Isa. 30:21)

The only thing that I can come up with is that those who say these things have never heard God's voice, because they are not tuned in. Perhaps they have never found Jesus as Lord and Savior. I know what I am implying. But by their own admission, they have stated that the Holy Spirit never told them that they were sinners. He never taught them the deep truths of God. He never has led them in paths of righteousness. Dear ones, I have just described what happens to people when they give their lives to Christ. When they become Christians, they begin to hear the voice of God, and for the rest of their lives, they hear that voice.

Froggie's little friend, Frogster, had been so very faithful. This little fella tried desperately to imitate everything Froggie did. And sure, here he was outside the institute—not sure what to do. His own parents' words resounded off the sides of his itty-bitty brain. "God intended you to be a frog. Don't get carried away with all Froggie's big notions. Someday, they will get you in trouble, and you'll end up on somebody's plate."

When Frogster mentioned this to Froggie, he received the worst tongue-lashing of his life. He had forgotten who Froggie was. He had forgotten how superior Froggie was to the rest of the frog world, and he was told in so many words to shut his mouth and go back to the dinky little pond that he had come from. He was told what a loser he was for not progressing into the next century.

"Frogster, you're a small-minded momma's frog, and you will never amount to nothing! You hear me. Stay out of the way because I am going forward to receive my destiny. I have potential, and I intend to let the 'god' of this age develop every bit of my special skills so the world will know…"

For it is by grace you have been saved, through faith—and this not from yourselves, it is the gift of God—not by works, so that no one can boast. For we are God's workmanship, created in Christ Jesus to do good works, which God prepared in advance for us to do. (Eph. 2:8–10)

My house shall be called a House of Prayer. (Matt. 21:13; Isa. 56:7)

What seems so amazing is the fact that God desires time-consuming, heart-wrenching, believing prayer. Everything that is accomplished in the kingdom is accomplished through prayer. We have traded prayer for technology. We feel that we are advancing the kingdom because of all the stuff we can do "worldwide." We don't need paper anymore, because we can send messages via e-mail. Wow! We saved a tree. (I thought we were to save people). We can have meetings without going to any certain place, and we can save gas (look at the money we saved!). I thought we were supposed to save *people*. We can send these messages, and we don't have to wait for the people to respond, and so we save time (I thought...). If only we would take all the "savings" and invest them in prayer to the God who *can* save us, we would save us a whole bunch of people and a whole lot of headaches. When is the last time you spent an hour in prayer? When is the last time you spent an hour on the computer? You do what you feel is important—always!

This technological advancement, called the
computer, stops dependence on God.

There are many who will disagree with my reasoning when it comes to dependency. During my alcoholism days before salvation, I learned about dependence. I didn't learn it from my psychology book, and I didn't learn it at a seminar. A theologian didn't explain the concept by teaching me in a classroom at the university. I learned it every time I went to the bar to "relieve" the stress. I learned it when I would try to kill the pain of my intense sufferings. I learned it when I and the good ol' boys wanted to go have a good time. But, folks, let me tell you...I learned from dependence that there was only one way to live properly. All things considered, I had to get rip-roaring drunk so that I could live properly. I depended on booze to get me through the day.

Look closer at who and what you depend on for everyday life. I am not a morning person, never have been and never will be. But, my friend, after thirty years of preaching the gospel, I have to get up much earlier than I did when I first started. Why? Because I know for a fact that *I can't handle the day no matter what it holds.* I also know that when people start to get up, my day will be interrupted; thus it is earlier and earlier that I pile out of the warm, cozy, little bed of mine. Now I have examined others quite closely. Some stay up late into the evening (night) so they can play games, send e-mails, or talk on Facebook or chat rooms. They even *shop* the network *until* they *drop*. Now they wake up the next morning (late) and claim they're not a morning person, never have been, never will be.

Look, you think I'm saying don't ever get on the computer. Wrong! My editor, if she will accept the assignment, will have to use the computer to straighten out this mess so that it makes sense. The dear lady who will make the cover for this book is so gifted at designing that you begin to see the story line before you even open the book. She will use the computer, and I will not tell her she has to use crayons or colored pencils. It's not about the tool; it is about the plan to draw you and me away from dependence on God to a dependence on something that will claim our time and our allegiance. Ultimately, it will draw us into a dependence on a man who has an evil intent for mankind. This will take place, and we won't know what happened to us. We will be given a delusion and be deceived into placing our trust in...

You need to grow up, my friend. Up until now, you have been telling me that the trap will not catch you, because of your spirituality. Great! But what about the millions of young people that are so, so, so dependent on the computer right now? Will that get any better? No! Everyone has a phone glued to their ear. They can hardly hold a conversation with a person right in front of them because they get a text message while talking to you and me. Don't you see that if you use snail mail you might receive the message that was intended for you and you might not? Technology is everything to this generation. They live and breathe for the next new thing out there. If I need it, I'll go search the web; and the web will bring me my desired gift, relationship, or instruction. That, my friend, is dependence. "I can't live without it." It's like a drug or being hypnotized. Well, looky here! That is the next generation that will run this country and the world as we know it. They will demand their way because they are being conditioned by technology, "rich or poor," "can't buy or sell," "a mark on the forehead or right hand." The young people will hate this message or just ignore what it has to say altogether. But you, friend, can't ignore it any longer. You've stayed on the computer a little too long and given them an example that okayed what they are doing. You must change your habits or be responsible for approving what they have gotten themselves into.

It's Not about the Tool. It's about the Plan.

Well, sure 'nuf! Ole Froggie got his wishes! Frogster left him all alone. And, believe it or not, the Palace (as Froggie liked to call it) was so much better than he had thought it would be. The enemy became his friend, the ponds were free of debris, and besides that, they were climate controlled. Deep in his conscience, he did feel a little sorrow that the Frogster hadn't come along. They had been together ever since they lost their tails and grew legs. Well, his loss! He had been told! Froggie guessed that he just didn't have the brainpower to realize how good it would be.

Maybe if he had only seen all the frogettes or the tons of flies…if he had had the chance to let the man gently carry him from one pond to another… I know this, Froggie began to realize that this was for him, and he wondered how he had ever got along without being here and having all this *advancement*!

He kind of depended on what good thing would happen next. Maybe someday when he got to his "position" in life, he would even send for Mom and Pop Frog. Maybe. Maybe not. Maybe they were still too small-minded, and maybe they were still depending on that stinky little ol' pond in the backwoods from so very long ago to accept the "gift."

Folks, you have to like ol' Froggie's thinking. Anything that is new and better has got to be good! It seems to look good from this vantage point! It sure seems like it will make the money so we can buy the necessities like food (and four cars and boats and big houses and trips around the world and...), and there just seems to be such a wealth of knowledge for the betterment of mankind. It sure seems dependable. What did we ever do without it?

To the Christians who are trying their dead-level best to stay true, this next area is...ah...well...so dangerous!

The Deception (Using the Tool) Catches Even the Innocent

Now, dear ones, when we look at this, area some are going to think along the lines outside of the church. But when I say *innocent*, it is meant to be all-inclusive. No one is exempt from the plan, and many will fall because of their own blind and deaf, selfish ways of instant gratification.

One of the most profound discoveries concerning the computer is the fact that many pastors (nationwide) fall to Internet pornography. When I first read this and wondered if it was fact or fiction, I began to question the Lord about how this could be possible. True to form, God had an illustration ready for me. One pastor told me that he had studied his theology via Internet. As he turned the page to read further, he discovered that a hacker had slipped a picture of a nude woman in a very provocative pose. While visiting this same pastor with another friend (another pastor), we were looking up something on the computer. As we scrolled down through a list of items to look at, the subject of mud wrestling appeared. Both pastors looked at each other and then asked what that was all about. Folks, I was hooked on porno when younger and knew instantly that it wasn't something to investigate and told them so. They laughed and went on. I still wasn't convinced until I found out that the first pastor was in trouble with his church for being on the website of pornography. He wasn't the first to be discovered, and he won't be the last.

These two men did not set out to do harm to their ministries. The plan didn't come from their minds even though it entered through their minds; and as James says, "The man is drawn away by his own lusts and enticed." The picture had to be presented to him, and then he had to make a decision. There is a plan to present "the picture" to every person on earth. To some, it's one picture; to another, something else. It will appeal to the heart of that individual pertaining to the sin that so easily besets that person. Did you know that there are ten thousands new porn sites being created ever day? Do you know how many young people visit those sites every day? Neither do I. But some of the stories I've heard would curl your hair. Young people being discovered and having the father defend those same children saying that it's okay to look at bizarre stuff on the Internet. And we wonder where the likes of Jeffry Dahmer come from!

I haven't mentioned all the killing games that hypnotize all the young people who play until late into the night and then act out the things they have learned. I didn't mention the people who meet others online only to drive miles to other cities so they can have an affair. I didn't mention the scams that are set up to steal money from well-intentioned folks. Did I mention that many who get involved are innocent and unsuspecting?

One friend sold his car via the Internet. It was a classic and worth a lot of money. So when it appeared for a very low price, someone from far away bought the car and sent the money so that no one else would get the good deal. Too bad it had been stolen off one website and transferred to another. Too bad it wasn't my friend that who doing the selling. Too bad there really wasn't any car at the second website.

Froggie wanted very much to get to the top rung of the ladder as fast as he could. So naturally, he would volunteer for every type of experiment that came along. He seemed to have his own little cheering section that shouted his name for all to hear. "Go, Froggie. Go, Froggie. You're the best."

He didn't realize that he didn't volunteer but rather went along with everything that had already been planned. In his quest to get out of life everything that he wanted, he missed the fact that he was being manipulated toward his own demise. Poor Froggie, if he had only listened... to Mom and Pop...to Frogster...to his girlfriend, Froggena...to his heart!

The tests were pretty "cool" when they first started. Froggie was lowered into a pond (he liked to call it a "spa," instead of a pond) of cold water. Now it was colder than he was used to, but to show how brave and how tough he was, he controlled his urge to leap from the "spa" back into the warm hands of his "friend." Well, self-control and the fact that he was a frog, his system didn't work so well in cold water. It didn't matter that he couldn't really show his stuff by swimming real fast. In fact, he couldn't swim at all. He seemed paralyzed. I think that his "man" saw his dilemma and turned the heat up just a little so that the pond got just a little warmer. After a while, Froggie was able to move a little, and it made him love that man so much more because of the care he had shown when Froggie was in trouble.

His innocence was taking him somewhere that he didn't want to go. But when you trust someone, you have to overlook a few things. It's for the betterment, *right?*

If you don't think that the innocent are being trapped, think about all the young girls who have lost their innocence because they just wanted someone to talk to. Scarred for life! Think of the ministries that have gone down the tubes because of a plan to cause them to fall into rotten garbage, not realizing that they would smell because of their involvement. Think of all the money that innocent people pour into lies that are told from cyberspace. If you refuse to think that it has a bearing on you and me, please think of the millions that are going to be suckered into getting their hand or forehead scarred for life...eternally paralyzed so they can't get out of the predicament that they find themselves in. Old folks who have to sign up for social security, thinking that it was just a number to secure their future. Now their future is being stolen from them, and the only way to get help is to continue to follow the plan. Not their plan—the plan the devil has had from the beginning. The plan to steal their freedom and destroy the relationship with a loving heavenly Father. The plan to destroy the relationships we have with good folks who care about our eternal destiny.

It's just like abuse in the home. It's just like a divorce between a man and a woman. The innocent child pays the price. And the innocent are still paying the price for our ignorance. We have treated it as if it didn't matter as long as we let technology...serve...us? I am afraid that we have missed the boat on this one. Rack your brain for just a skinny minute, and ask yourself, Who is serving whom? Can't you feel the net tightening around humanity? Can't you see that we are being drawn in? A lot of innocent people will die and go to hell because we played the game by someone else's rules, too dumb to fight back, too dumb to realize that we had been sucker punched and are going down for the count. After all, we are intelligent people, aren't we?

I mentioned earlier that the children of Israel wanted a tangible God. It's true, you know. Humanity hasn't changed in all these years. They still want a god they can see or touch or feel.

Ask yourself this question: Why do people say that they can feel the presence of the Lord in this or that service? Don't just give me the answer you're comfortable with. Look at it with open eyes. Every time I have ever heard that, it happened when the music was just right or the preacher spoke in such a way that pleased us. It was when the program seemed pleasing and made us feel good. Come on now, don't back up on me. If you're truthful with me, you acknowl-edge that at that moment of time, it made you feel warm and fuzzy or perhaps made you cry. Maybe it pleased you with the appeal to the eye. They (or it) looked good, and that pleased you also.

Tangible gods come in many forms. Dress-it-up lipstick, cool clothes, and snazzy sparkles, and just about anybody will buy it. Why do you think people spend millions of dollars on advertisements? Because they know that if they package it right, the money will start to roll in. The computer is no different. It packages everything that will get your attention so that you will continue to come back or perhaps look into it.

Some of it is shocking but presented in such a way as to get your attention and sooner or later your allegiance. Some appeal to the lust within your eyes (not always concerning sexual things), but we have to see more. The more we see, the more we want to see. Pretty soon we sit before our tangible god hypnotized into believing it is a god, and we begin to think that it has all our answers. You say no. I say why then does everything have to be changed so that it becomes computerized? I can't have a conversation with my relatives until I interrupt them from whatever form of computer they are on. Auuummm, auuummm, oh, great one! We bow before your throne and give you our allegiance, our time, our energy, our resources, our money, our hearts… The pious ones within the church will scream out loud and give excuses that we just need to control our technology and our kids. *Is it working?* Quit being so self-centered, and look at the masses. Your kids are little models of what Christianity should look like. But what about the masses that don't even want to hear the answer to their problems, the ones who run away from home because no one seems to care within that home, and the ones who are so hooked on what the computer can do for them that they hate anyone who tries to tell them to control their use of time? What about the rise in teen suicide? One girl committed suicide because her parents took away her cell phone. What about the rise in gambling? I receive advertisements for casinos, online gambling, and the lottery. Don't even go there! The lottery is a legalized form of the numbers racket from the '20s and '30s back in the 1900s. Now it is computerized so that we have the hope of winning millions. What about…? Get real! A chip in the pet, in the car, in our hand, or on our forehead!

Get real! Win a million, lose a granddaughter. Win a trip, lose a wife. Win recognition on MySpace, and lose my identity, perhaps in more ways than one.

> At first, Froggie thought that the cage was for his protection, you know, to keep the varmints out. Now he did wonder, *What varmints?* At first, he did wonder what the little wristband was for. He had thought it to be a bracelet to let all the other frogs know how important he was. Lately, he had noticed that all the other frogs had "bracelets" too. At first, he thought the man was his friend, but lately he had seen him handle all the other frogs the same way. Slip them out of their cage. Slip them into a pool of water. Slip them out of the pool of water. Slip them into their cage. Maybe it was just a touch of home-sickness or the fact that he was tired of dead flies or that he no longer got to play with the frogettes. His eyes couldn't have deceived him, now, could they? He was going places, wasn't he? Everything looked so appealing…back then. Surely his brain hadn't given him wrong information about what was happening!

So much of the time we see something that we think would benefit our lives, so we choose to throw caution to the wind. We quit listening to the voice of God with these thoughts in mind: This will do what I need it to do, so life will be better; and, secondly, there is no other alternative—it is the age we live in. We are sort of like the young man in chapter 7 of Proverbs who follows after the adulterous woman. We just don't realize that this is going to cost us our life. We fail to look into the future and what might be coming.

If I were belittling the computer because I was so old and didn't want to learn anything new, okay. If I didn't have Internet, personally, because I was afraid of getting trapped into porno, okay. But two things are happening as I am writing this book:

The God of the universe has impressed my mind with information that a trap was being set to capture my soul. It isn't just about discipline or self-control in my life. It isn't just a haphazard plan that may trap a few. It is a calculated plan that will cause the very elect to fall, if that were possible. A last-minute push to discredit God and all his children. A plan that will spit one last time in the face of Jesus and his redemptive grace.

The second thing is that more and more I am seeing my friends and family being drawn into Facebook, e-mail, texting, buying and selling, and seemingly having to do everything by the computer whether they want to or not. It has consumed their time, it has sapped their energy, and it has interrupted their ability to communicate with each other on a personal level.

You say, "What an odd, undisciplined family you have." I say, "Wake up and smell the coffee! *It is the norm! It is getting worse and worse, and it is not going to get any better!*"

The Last Mile of the Way, Forgive Me for Not Listening!

We will blame Eve (the men especially will) for as long as we live. She was tempted by that ol' slippery serpent and fell for the lies that he told her. Most people look at her and mutter things like "Why was she so stupid?" or "If she had only resisted that one time!" What we don't see because of the way the Bible is constructed is that for the perfect couple to fall, the temptation didn't just happen in one day as the serpent was walking by. Yes, he was walking until the fall. Read it for yourself in chapter 3 of Genesis. Many a day the plan just slipped in place, and the man and woman just sat back and ignored the subtle suggestions that Satan had made. They loved their garden, and they loved their God, and they loved each other.

The serpent wasn't any more than a beautiful animal that happened by every day or so. What he had to say wasn't bold and brash with a demand that they break all contact with God and break the one and only commandment that God had given them. Subtle, oh, so subtle! "That's a nice-looking piece of fruit!" and he wasn't even talking about the tree of knowledge of good and evil. In fact, if he tempted them the way he has tempted me, he showed them every tree in the garden before he showed them *the* tree. Why, he wanted to engage them in conversation, and he wanted to get them to trust that he was not a threat to each other and to their relationship to God.

I also believe that he was crafty enough to know that he would get many rejections before the trap would work. He had battled the Father before and knew that he must wait until the right moment to spring the trap so that he could catch the prey. He knew he couldn't whip the Holy Trinity, so he chose God's creation. Yes, friend, you and me!

Froggie didn't get any more cold baths for a long time. Just zombie-type living. Cage—pond. Pond—cage. See your friends—yeah...from a distance! No real communications—just the same saddened eyes that he felt he had. It had gotten so bad that no one even waved anymore. It wasn't fun to zoom around the pond anymore.

And the dreams! Oh, the dreams! Night after night, it was the same ol' thing. The dreams always took him back to the good ol' days where he and Frogette and Frogster had played in the good ol' pond. The place where he could eat good ol' live flies. The place where his heart would beat so fast and hard because that humongous good ol' bass had tried to swallow him. Where he sat on the good ol' bank with Mom and Pop and talked about everything and yet talked about nothing. It's odd, but it began to be a nightmare 'cause every time he had to wake up and find himself in that cold, dark cage with no one to talk to. No real personal contact with anyone. If only something would happen to wake him from this terrible dream!

Now I know for a fact that many don't want to go back to the good ol' days. There are a lot of good reasons that we don't want to. The peach tree switch you had to cut. Where I'm living, to pick cotton by hand. The flour sacks that we had to wear. The one egg for the whole family to eat. But let me say a few things about that. They were hard days with smelly ol' outhouse toilets, but did we take pills by the handful back then? High blood pressure, heart attacks, nervous conditions. There is an epidemic of people taking pills for depression. I, for one, have fought all my life with depression but wouldn't give in to the doctor's request for medication because my mother committed suicide with prescribed medication. Mask the problem, serve the symptom. Forget the all-powerful, healing Savior. I don't have a problem with it anymore. Yes, it took years for him to uncover the problem. For me, it was unforgiveness.

Back then, we didn't have much money, but we didn't have the money problems we have today. The credit card hadn't come into existence. We didn't buy houses way beyond our ability to pay for. We made an honest living with hard work and paid our bills as best we could. We didn't go do stuff "just because." What I'm telling y'all is that, even though you and I don't want to go backward, we know that there were some things that we wish we had back or could do again. We seem so trapped into believing that this is the way it should be, that we can't see what we have lost. We can't see how much damage we have done to our society, to our homes, and to our health. Yes, we admit it. But all we do about it is to treat the symptom. Give me another pill…give me another job…give me more pleasure…give me more technology…

I noticed the other day on the news that the ballplayers who make millions were suing for money they should have made when in college playing ball. I believe they are trying to set a precedent for future ballplayers. Too bad everything has to be about money… You can only serve one master, ya know.

Our government may have to shut down for lack of funds. Funny, ain't it, that we can bail out everyone else but we can't bail ourselves out of debt—at least with borrowed money! Back yonder, we didn't continue to borrow when we needed more. We waited.

We worked. We didn't overspend—most of the time. Don't argue because of your bad habits! Fess up and tell the truth! You don't want to go back to the ol' ways, because you would have to give up some of your stuff and some of your lifestyles. You don't want to acknowledge that you are taking pills to help you go to sleep at night, to wake up in the morning, to get energy to make it through the day. You don't want to admit that you have more than one job to support so many unnecessary items that you have around your house or that you play the lottery with the thought that you will someday hit it big so you can get out of debt.

We seem to make excuses to justify everything that is wrong today. Our government has gone wacko. Our families have disintegrated. Our economy is failing. There aren't enough jobs (especially at the lower end of the spectrum without computer skills). Even though we live longer, our health has fallen apart.

I'm not painting a dismal picture! I'm telling the truth! In the most advanced age anyone has ever lived in, I must say that we are in a mess, and we know it! Our biggest problem is that we have forgotten our Creator and what he has done for those he created. We can't memorize a verse from his Word, but we memorize a thousand ways to get into the computer and find things that we shouldn't be finding. We can't get up on Sunday morning, but we can stay awake half the night to send messages about nonsense that has no real meaning. We blame anyone and everyone and refuse to take our share of the responsibility for what has gone wrong. It's the rotten government's fault, it's the teachers' fault, it's big business that is at fault, it's the sinful nature that is at fault…but it is not our fault?

> On his best day, Froggie felt that if he could just croak, he would be better off. Frogs don't have tear ducts, but it sure seemed like there were little rivulets of water coursing down his green cheeks. If only there could be just a little bit of excitement in his day…!
>
> It didn't feel like he had any energy today to swim around in his man-made pond. (He had

ceased to call it a spa, for it gave no comfort at all.) Nevertheless, there was the man, just like always, opening his cage, grabbing hold of his slimy little body down the hall and into the pond room. At least, it didn't look like he was going to be eased into the water today. He remembered the day of the cold bath he had taken. The man had dropped him in from about two feet up from the pond. This was some of the only excitement going these days. Wait! The heater is on today, so at least it won't be cold! Here we go… Ahhh! Helppp! Yowww!

Before he knew what had happened, Froggie had jumped completely out of the pond and sat trembling on the metal table that surrounded the pond. His tired muscles had come to life and responded to some very hot water. His skin was now pink, his heart was beating out of control, and his mind was reeling with thoughts about his man doing something like this to him! How could it happen? Why would he do such an awful thing to someone he loved?

I guess Froggie shook for over an hour. He certainly was glad for the bars to protect him. He was glad that he was alone so the others couldn't see the fear in his eyes. After all, he was King Frog from Podunk Pond, wasn't he? I know this—he didn't dream on that night. In fact, he didn't even sleep that night. How could he? He had been abused and misused!

Backed into the recesses of his cage, he began to think about what had happened. Maybe the man had just goofed up and put too much heat. As a matter of fact, he probably was just try-ing to make things comfortable for him. Maybe his assistant made the mistake and didn't tell the man how long the heat had been on. Froggie began to relax and finally sleep… Zzz!

It's odd, ain't it? Froggie never once thought that it was his bad choice that got him into hot water. No, sir, it was not his fault! Mom and Pop maybe… They never would let him have enough freedom. Maybe the elders of the pond back home… You and I both know that they made too many rules to follow. Maybe it was God's fault (if there is a god). If he had just given a little more of this and that and hadn't made the pond…well, you know…

It's so amazing, isn't it? Mankind is so advanced! There is hardly anything that he doesn't know or anything that he can't find out. But there are two things that he has yet to discover. One, he won't admit that he is in trouble. Secondly, he won't confess that he is part of the problem. His pride in what he has accomplished and who he is overwhelms his brain and convinces him that everything is all right.

He doesn't realize that greed at the top began with greed at the bottom. He doesn't realize that porn makers started with the little man wanting something dirty to look at. Pastors don't realize that because of their determination to have it their way, the church splits. (Half agreed with them to their own demise.) A politician doesn't realize that the problems stem from their own greedy, selfish desires that tax people unfairly and govern harshly. Instead, we complain and rail against each other and expect revival and renewal if the other group would get their act together.

We are a lot like the Fonz on *Happy Days*. We just can't seem to say, "We're wro…wron…wrong." We can't seem to say that we are sorry. And maybe if we *are* sorry, it's sorry that we got caught or sorry that we do find ourselves in a mess that we can't get out of. Maybe, just maybe, if we would take the blame down on our level for the poor decisions we make things would get back to the way they used to be. Maybe, just maybe, if we would confess that we are part of the problem and stop complaining about the other fella, we would get back to God and his redemptive power through Jesus Christ. It's our only hope! It's our only chance of getting out of this world alive!

Fuss and Fume All You Want. He Is Still God!

Fuss and fume at me for writing this crazy book if you want. I know he told me to write this; and I know that this crusty, technologically challenged, ol' buzzard would rather have you rail against me than have the God of the universe be dissatisfied with my lack of willingness to be obedient. It will be his smile that will thrill my soul, not yours.

Let's compare notes for a minute. Let's compare the God of the universe with the computer. Quit fussing and keep reading.

God is all-knowing.

From the beginning of time to the present, there is not one little thing, thought, or happening that has come into existence that God didn't or even now doesn't know about. I don't know how he did and does that, but it is true. I'm not convinced because of what others tell me; I'm convinced because of the many, many times he has proven that he knows all there is to know about everything. And listen, now that I'm older, even what I claim to know, I seem to forget. Someone may say to me, "Do you remember this or that?" Was it yesterday? No, I don't remember. God never forgets.

I have a pastor friend who had gone to Vietnam before Christ had come into his heart. He found himself in a no-win firefight with the Viet Cong. As one of the only members left in his platoon, trapped under a bridge, he made the pledge to the Lord God "that if he would deliver him from his deadly peril, he would preach his word." Folks, he wasn't even a Christian. God had not forgotten that he was trapped under that bridge, and he didn't forget that he had given conditions when he had prayed. My friend is now the pastor of the church we were saved in.

How can God keep all these facts together? How can he know all the facts before they are needed? Some things are planned out, you know, in preparation for what is needed in the future. I could go on a long time about that one. If you're honest with yourself, you could fill in a lot of those blanks and would be very surprised at what had been accomplished without your knowing what was needed in the future.

If we would look into all of creation, we would discover a vast array of designs that would baffle the mind. The cosmic holds no bars when it comes to creativity. Billions of stars, many galaxies, and more unanswered questions than you could shake a stick at show that it took a great intellectual mind to conceive all that has been made. If we look more closely, we see a molecular system that is so complex that the scientists are still discovering new horizons. I'm not going to try to give many examples or statistics so that you will be overly impressed. I'm not smart enough. But I have seen my babies born and know that it took a lot of knowledge to get a baby to swim underwater for nine months and then come bursting into life and begin to cry at the top of their lungs so their birth will be noticed. I've gone out at night and looked at the stars on the side of the hill at my brother-in-law's and was overwhelmed at the sight (he lives where there are few external lights).

I've also had smart people show me the things in the universe that I cannot see. It's so much more than I could possibly imagine. I could relay a few of the details but not many. I do know that I am awestruck by what they tell me and what I can see. It didn't just happen because of some cosmic, random explosion. It wasn't by chance. There had to be a great mind with more knowledge behind it than could be explained by mere humans who are still discovering. For you to disagree with my synopsis of the matter is crazy. If we know so much, why are we still trying to explain what we still can't fully understand? God is the all-knowing One, and even science will prove that to be true.

If you can explain *almost* all of it, you are not God.

The one thing that I know is that he knows you, when you get up in the morning, when you go to bed at night, and what you do all through the day.

The computer knows an awful lot, now, doesn't it?

When the techs try to explain things to me, I get very lost, very quickly. I usually tell them that I can't understand, and they look at me like I am ignorant. I am, and I am not afraid to admit it. I went to buy a laptop the other day (the *plan* is the problem, not the tool!), and the guy used some fancy language to tell me which one I needed. When I explained to him that I needed an explanation, he told me that I needed the one with two brains so it wouldn't have to work so hard. It was crystal clear like mud at that moment of time, so I thanked him and went on. If the computer is so smart, why does it need two brains? I have one, and I get along fine—*sometimes*.

I have to admit that the medical field has advanced tremendously when it comes to diagnosing deceases. Send in the information, and out come the possibilities. Performing an operation can be had without all the slicing and dicing. Turn it over to a computer and shazam!—the computer operates with pinpoint accuracy without ever entering the body the old-fashioned way of blood and guts.

I have a farmer friend who bought the newest technology. He put this system in and omitted at least two people. The machines are now guided by a satellite. When he plants, he programs the coordinates of the field, and when time to harvest comes, he doesn't even have to drive the tractor. It already knows the exact trail to follow, so the harvest is down to inches of the path taken to plant. Then the combine packages the crop while it is still on the machine. The only thing that has to be done anymore is turn the machine around every now and then and tell someone to come and get the crop. Amazing!

There is so much advancement that for me to try to tell this age what the computer knows and knows how to do would make a fool out of me. I don't know the half of what is going on in our modern world today. They can tell you who you are by looking into your eye. They have refrigerators that can tell you when you're out of groceries and then order them for you. They have smart bombs that can hit a target within the inch. You can send messages all over the world, and everyone is doing it all at the same time, and you don't even need wires. It's all floating around depending on the computer to attract the message to the right computer to the right person. Amazing!

There are several things that can't be done with the computer. I left mine on the other day, and when I came back, not one word had been written so this book could be completed sooner. It can't do what it has not been programmed to do. It has to be told what to do, and no matter how advanced things get, this will always be true.

The other thing that is true about the computer is that it can't choose what is good and what is evil. It is impartial to the material that is submitted to it. And that's the reason that I compare it to the tree of good and evil. It has both contained within, and it has no heart to say this is wrong and this is right. It has no wisdom to say that this is hurtful and this is helpful. Man is the one that puts out the information and the determinations of what is wrong and what is right. And, friend, there is a great battle going on to see who is right!

It was so amazing to see what happened after the "incident"! Things began to cool down for Froggie. He was given "pool time" with his friends. There were live flies to catch and eat. The man even seemed to have the water in the pond heated to the right temperature for once. Now don't be fooled! It took Froggie a long time to get his nerves back under control. His trust system in regard to the man was sketchy at best.

Froggie examined every little detail when taken out of the cage. Was there steam coming off the pond? Were there other frogs to "play" with? How high above the water was Froggie when the man let him go? Yet week after week, the man gained Froggie's trust back. Well, it wasn't so much trust as it was…could you say…lulled back to thinking about the good time he was having or perhaps thinking about the "girl" frogs that were in the pond that day that called him "Prince Charming," "Cutie Pie," or "Darling."

Things were returning to the way it was when he first came to the place of higher learning. It was finally turning out the way he had thought it would…

"Gravy Train Special"!

I call what is happening to our world these days the leapfrog effect. We're handed something that is so utterly evil that it shocks our system and outrages our mind. We fuss and fume about it for a while and things are corrected, or so it seems. We live at peace for a while, and then something just a little bit worse than the first shock comes along. This second shock jumps completely over the first shock, and we become outraged at the second shock. We fuss and fume until we get those that perpetrated the second shock to recant. But while we are fussing about the second shock, the first shock is installed in place with a little bit of *permanency*. Then the third shock is introduced…

Let me give you some examples of what I am talking about. There was a show that came on TV, and the main characters depicted lifestyles that are contrary to Christian living. The Christian community was outraged and lobbied against the show. Well, the show didn't last long, and the Christian community simmered down, and all was fine. In about a year or so, the *Temptations of Christ* came out, depicting that Jesus had affairs with women and such. Here we go again! The Christian community got in an uproar. The characters of the first show were silently slipped in while the Christians fought on this new front. Those types of shows of the first shock are now the norm, and we don't say anything about them. Oh, we may mutter a little bit but no real showing out like before.

Let me show you a bit bigger picture. The TV was introduced, and it was called evil. It was going to destroy society. Let it simmer for a while. Throw the dog a bone every once in a while. Elvis, you can't shake your hips on TV, because some think that it's obscene. Have you ever watched *Dancing with the Stars*? They shake more than their hips!

Anyway, we finally got used to the TV, so now the computer is introduced. Some say that it is the devil's tool to destroy or take captive mankind. You know, they said it about the TV, and the TV never hurt us? Well, yes, it did, and you know it!

Now we have a tool that is programmed with intent. Sucker people in with good things, and then place alongside a host of things that are intrinsically evil, and let them make the choice. Call it good, call it helpful, and then watch them destroy themselves. Are you still so blind that you can't see what is happening?

Secondly, the Social Security System was looked at as evil. They are not going to number me! It may be the mark of the beast! I sent in for my Social Security this last month. Hopefully, it isn't the mark of the beast, but just think about it for a minute. Someone has cultivated your mind and the mind of your children and grandchildren for many years. Not just with Social Security but with the credit card, the debit card, and the checking account. Friend, the Social Security System is in big trouble, and you've heard for years that the benefits are going to go away. Our lifestyle has prepared this nation to see it happening but has lulled us to sleep so that we don't prepare ourselves for the eventual outcome. It will happen. Just you wait and see.

Here is the whole of it. Am I going to trust in a system of any sort that is created by man with limited knowledge, or am I going to believe that there is an all-knowing God who is willing to guide me through these last days? I can stick my head in the sand and pretend that it won't happen, or I can deepen my faith in the finished work of Jesus Christ and the ongoing work of the Holy Spirit, my Guide. To do the latter, I will have to decide who is all-knowing and who is to have more and more of my time, more of my mind, and more of my dependency. The one thing that I can't do is to be lulled to sleep because of the many gimmicks that proceed from this age of technology. The tool will lead us on a path that we don't really want to go down, because of a plan that has been set in motion. That plan is for our destruction by making us captive to allegiance to another. *God is all powerful, always has been, always will be!*

If Satan plans to move us to the place where we can't buy or sell, we know he has some work to do. First, he must convince us that

God is either nonexistent, dead, or too weak to carry us through. Biblically, we see the enemy being defeated when victory should have been theirs. Gideon faced the Midianites with three hundred men. The enemy, on the other hand, had thousands and thousands of fighting men. God gave the directions, and God gave the victory. David, as a young man, faced a giant nine feet, nine inches tall. God gave the instructions; God gave the victory. The people of Israel were holed up inside the city without any food. God said, "Wait and see." The next day 185,000 Assyrians were dead, and the people of the city went out found all the food that was needed for everybody. They crucified the Son of God and stuffed him into a musty, dark ol' tomb. Three days later, God the Father raised him from the dead.

There is no telling how many stories could be referred to within the confines of the Bible. Every one of them helps my faith to grow. But like Froggie, I live in the here and now. I want to know that God is not dead or asleep or too old. I want to know that he is still all-powerful in my day and age. I just want you to know that he, God, has not disappointed me in any way, shape, or form. I had become an alcoholic and drunk, but one day in a bar, God steps on the scene; and not only does he call me out of the bar, but he sets me free from alcoholism (that day)! My son becomes a drug addict—using crystal meth, cocaine, and booze. God shows up, and in one day, Jeff is delivered from the whole mess! My wife accidentally, with the help of our two-year-old grandson, runs into our church at forty miles per hour on a four-wheeler. She T-boned it and hit head-on. There was no sign of life until God shows up and brings her back from the dead. My friend, I have so many stories that could have been disastrous except that God showed up in his all-powerful form and routed the enemy. Victory was the outcome every time!

Whether it is a Bible story or personal things that God has done for my family and me, it makes no difference. It stands that he is all-powerful. I've seen that same thing happen on the world stage as well. When we line up with his Word, the outcome will be victory! The six-day war in the Middle East and the Arab nations defeated by the little country of Israel. There was no hope except that God showed up. Even before that Hitler had tried to take over the world, and in the midst of the commotion, Israel became a nation. The impossible made possible. When there is no hope, he has given hope.

The computer thinks it is all-knowing. What kind of statement is that?

I have to give fair credence to the computer. There are so many things that the computer can do. It can wake us up in the morning. It can start things going before we are awake. It can give us messages that have been out there in cyberspace. It can find our lost pet or keys or cars or...

I do know that my granddaughter had come up missing, and because of the computer/telephone, my daughter found her 1,200 miles away. That happened in one day. Fly out, pray, look at the list (online) of phone calls (where they had been made from), pray... There she is...standing with a group of ten other people her age (whole other story that isn't finished yet). The truth is that the *computer* made finding the granddaughter possible. Finding the granddaughter—maybe that was an answer to prayer. You be the judge, if you dare.

One of the things that I have found exciting is that the computer has caught more criminals red-handed than any time in history. I sure wouldn't want to do bad things in today's time. Fingerprinting, DNA, last seen...the list goes beyond my comprehension. I know that it is a valuable tool that catches these crooks red-handed, and I am glad.

How all-powerful is the machine that can tally, keep track of, and send instant messages around the world; find things that we lost; start and end wars; and discover stuff that is helpful to mankind? Check it out! I have just discovered the god of this age. For years, we have tried to claim that man, within himself, was God, his potential, his ability, his strength, his insight, his resources, his power. All of a sudden, it has become clear to me. Everything that the computer knows was put there by man. Now I know why we like it so much and defend it to the ends of the earth. The computer represents how great man is and how he can solve the problems of the world. It represents all of his knowledge, and every accomplishment represents how able man is. That has got to be why Satan can use this tool so well for man's destruction. Man's pride draws him along because of the imagination that sets mankind to be the *"man."* This book isn't about fighting technology, because I'm old and antiquated. This book isn't about fighting progress. This book isn't about contesting smart people versus dumb people. This book is about the battle between God and man with his sinful, puny, prideful heart. This book is about why you, my friend, bristle every time I say that the computer is the great delusion sent by God. He has given us the desires of our heart: *"Let me be god, and I will show you what I can do."*

From the day Froggie entered into the "palace," he wondered about something that would take place. The man, whom he had thought to be a friend, would carry around this clipboard. From the beginning, Froggie was measured and weighed and examined. Of course, Froggie loved the attention, and his mind worked overtime to figure out why the man was doing this.

It must have had something to do with what a great frog Froggie was! He liked to think that the man would show all the other men and all the other frogs what a fine specimen he was. You know—longest legs, the greatest weight (for a frog that is good), the biggest head (to house a great brain). Maybe it was just his imagination, but his head kept getting bigger and bigger because of what he imagined. His accomplishments were going to show the world what greatness really is! His presence would give the world something to shoot for so they could be just like him! His knowledge was going to show the world how to think so that progress could reach its ultimate goal—that of thinking just like Froggie!

Too bad Froggie was so stuck on himself. That fact alone stopped him from seeing clearly what was happening to him.

Too bad our imagination gets so much of our time. It tells us that our computer is a great time-saving device, yet we have less and less time for prayer. Too bad our imagination uses so much of our energy; it tells us that we will be in better condition because we learn new things. Too bad we can't learn new things within the Scripture. You do know, don't you, that there is no end to the depth of the Bible, for it is the Word of God, and there is no end to the depth of God? Too bad our imagination tells us that we are so smart and that we can learn new stuff about our world every day. Too bad we don't realize that there is nothing new under the sun. It has been discovered before and forgotten. Don't argue with me; that's what the Bible says.

I just wish that we would learn from our mistakes. The Tower of Babel was not an accomplishment by man. The Tower of Babel caused division between men. The Tower of Babel caused confusion between men as they tried to communicate. God had seen how high and mighty man was becoming. He knew that they thought they could touch God because of their accomplishments, so he dispersed them around the world and confused their language. Why won't we learn from their mistake?

Adam and Eve thought they were smarter than God. Everything had been given to them that would give life and happiness. Yet they chose to believe that they knew best. Eating the "apple" wouldn't hurt this one time. Eating from the tree that God said not to eat from wouldn't hurt this one time. Eating from the tree of knowledge of good and evil won't hurt, because it will make us more godlike. The tree of good and evil is the wealth of knowledge that sums all things up. The computer will lead us to the man who sets himself up as god, and he will claim to have all knowledge and all power. Read 2 Thessalonians 2 for yourselves. It's all there for the taking. It's there for the eating, for it is soul food for your soul. The Word of God gives all things pertaining to life. Nothing can be added. Nothing! It's the most powerful thing in the universe anywhere! Our pride is the only thing that will lead us down the wrong path.

God is everywhere present—always has been, always will be.

I don't even know how to start this. I can't "see" God at this moment of time, and actually, I have never seen God. So how can I say that he is everywhere present? I am going to state that as a fact, anyway. God is everywhere present.

If I were to reason it out, I would have to say that if he created all that is, he has a capability that can't be comprehended. You know as well as I that the universe stretches out there for quite a ways. It wouldn't take much of an imagination to see that if he wasn't everywhere present; he would still be out there building something, trying to get back for the next project. And another thing, if he listens to our prayers, and there are quite a few people praying, he would have to tell some of them to wait just a minute because he was listening to someone else. He has to be everywhere present for him to listen and answer all the requests that are made.

Take for instance, when my wife hit the wall with our four-wheeler and at that exact time someone feels the need to pray for her, what do you think? Do you think that he wasn't in two places at once? Now if he can do that, why do we have a problem with seeing him everywhere? How could the other person know that Di needed prayer? It's happened all over the world with so many situations that it would make an unbeliever believe if they would just shut up and listen and think for just a minute.

The computer is everywhere present—never has been and
never will be. (Sorry, I just had to put in my two cents.)

With satellites and computer technology, there seem to be fewer and fewer places we can go to hide. I want you to know right out and out, I am in over my head at this moment of time. I don't know all that the computer can do pertaining to the knowing where everything and everybody is. But the good news is, I know a little. I know that there are TVs out there that can tell how many people are in the house and may even be able to tell what you have been watching on any given day. I know that with OnStar, if you're in an accident, it can send a wrecker to the exact location. I know that when people are on house arrest, they can put a bracelet on your leg, and they will know if you leave the house. I also know that if they were to place a chip in your right hand or in your forehead, they could follow you to the ends of the earth. You could not run and hide.

It is sort of like the parent who cared enough to follow their child with their mind. The parent would know where the child was without even having to be there. Now look at what I just said. The parent would know but won't be there. They were guessing but not actually present. Now look at the computer for just a minute. It is just about everywhere. I like to kid about people calling me at various places and then wonder how they knew that I was at that particular location. My cell phone (handheld computer) told them. Computers are being used in some very remote places in this modern world we live in. But consider for a minute, it is not everywhere. In the remote jungle of Africa, there is no computer. Take that same location, and you will find that God has visited (shown that he is there), and people get saved.

I'm trying to get you to see that the dark world is trying to take their little instrument and keep close track of where you are and what you are doing. When you begin to see that the friendlier you are with the instrument, the easier it will be for the darkness to keep the light from you. With that being said, the easier it will be to put a mark on your right hand or your forehead. You just don't get it, do you?

Froggie wondered also about the man he called friend. Look at him. He has the power to take care of this whole place. He brings the food. He changes the water. He cares for all these frogs. Why, even if one were to croak, the man is the one to bury them. Froggie never was one to be awestruck with someone else. But this man, this man was something who could be admired. Oh, Froggie still remembered the hot-water incident. But, hey, everyone is entitled to one mistake!

Let's face it. It had come to the fact that the one he could trust the most was the man. He seemed to have more power than anyone else. He seemed to know more than anyone else. Maybe he was the one that they call god. After all, look how big he is. He is huge! If he needs a new pond for other frogs, he just creates them. If he needs more flies for more frogs, he just sends some of his servants (maybe they are angels) to go get them.

The more Froggie talked to himself, the more convinced he was that everything was going to be all right. That inclined him to trust the human more. Maybe he didn't make such a bad mistake after all! Maybe he will be crowned king after all!

Froggie is just so naïve that he really thinks everything is going to be okay. I would venture a guess that we are not far behind him. We, or many, say that we are in deep trouble. But to tell you the truth, we act like there is nothing wrong and we don't have a thing to worry about. I'm told to sound the alarm, and with everything I have within me, that is what I am trying to do. Business as usual. Go to work and make as much money as you can. The economy will turn around anytime now. Go here and there, and seek as much pleasure as possible. No one is trying to get me to conform so they can take over the world. It's just a bunch of crooked politicians being stupid!

God is all-caring.

If you don't have a relationship with him through Jesus Christ, I won't convince you that he cares. If you have a relationship with him, I can try to encourage you to seek him in greater ways so you will find out that he does care for you with more love and compassion than you could ask for or imagine. He sent his "only begotten Son" to die on a death stick called the cross just so you could be saved from an eternal death in the hell fires that will burn forever. He has given his word, and He won't retract it no matter what happens. He will never leave you nor forsake you.

It won't mean as much to you as it does to me, but there have been hundreds of times when God has shown me how much he cares for me and for my family. When all is lost for health reasons, he has been there. When money is needed in so many ways, he has been able to supply what is needed. When directions are needed about where to go next, he is there to show me the way. My salvation is the greatest show of his care, but his ongoing persistence in caring is what has brought me through the deepest of valleys.

The computer is caring.

Maybe you are one of those dear people who imagine that your computer is absolutely brilliant, that the computer is an instrument of knowledge, there is no doubt. But far from going into a lot of detail, it (or the people who design and program the machine) does not care a frog's leg about you. Before you launch into a tirade about how wrong I am, stop for a second and listen. Most of those people who advertise all the benefits that the product will give you are now millionaires or more. They became that way because they sold their product with a high markup on the price. Next, they never did get to know you, because you're just a consumer, the twenty thousandth sale this month providing a profit margin of 75 percent. Well, friend, if you know that much, you should also know that the product, which is inanimate, doesn't give a rip about who you are.

There is also the side that talks about the trouble the computer can get you into. It can bill you too much, too many times, without caring anything about your little bitty feelings. It doesn't care if you get on to the wrong site and it harms your heart or brain. It doesn't care if you meet someone online and it turns into an affair and you lose your marriage. It doesn't care if your teenage son plays so many war games that he begins to act them out and ends up killing some- one. It doesn't care if your children become mindless and can't do anything but play on the computer all day and all night. It could care less! Why? Because the plan that is behind the tool is to draw you in and then destroy your Christianity. It will make all things impersonal and then hypnotize you so that you step in line. After all, what is a chip in the hand if it will keep someone from stealing your credit card? Why not put one in your forehead if it will keep someone from breaking into your bank account and stealing your checks? What will be claimed for your safety will end up for your destruction—all for a loaf of bread, a polished new car, or the feeling that you are now in the know!

Prison talk had it that one of the frogs from down the line had been bad so they boiled him to death. First, Froggie didn't realize that he had switched to calling this place a prison. Secondly, if the boiling had taken place, the frog had to be one of those who were in the way of progress. It had woken him up to some very important facts. Instead of hiding in the back of the cage, partly because of sadness, partly because of fear, Froggie now met the man at the front of the cage. He would leap into the hands of the man with all the power. He knew one thing very well: he didn't want to do anything to make the caretaker of his life mad. Mind you, this was just a precaution that just may save his life.

People will do just about anything to appease the one that may have power over them. We do a lot of complaining, mind you. But when the cards are on the table, let's not push too hard so that we get ourselves in too much trouble. They do have the power, you know. Yes, there are a few rabble-rousers who will buck the system. But when faced with jail time or faced with a stiff fine, most will conform. Don't stand up, or you might get knocked down. Fear is the equalizer in this equation. Fear of being rejected. Fear of being made fun of. Fear of the unknown of what could happen to you. Fear that there is no God to care for you.

Delusion, Detour, Demise

We have a lot of illegal drugs in our area. (I guess everyone does nowadays.) Twenty-eight people were arrested the other day when a sting operation went down. Some, it is said, have been doing this for years and years. I assume that they never intended to get caught, and now they are facing federal charges that could send them away for a long time. Lots of drugs, piles of money, cars and boats, as well as freedom, gone in a moment of time. What could possibly make people chance the risk of getting caught and sent away to prison? What could make people continue when they had watched others take the same route? Greed? Perhaps. Prestige? Maybe. The excitement? Could be. Just as likely, the demon spirits that control the drug industry appealed to the inner nature of those men and women and perhaps used all of the above.

If I look at many of those who got caught, I see also that they had something in common. They were injured people needing recognition. There was no one to care for them and cause them to feel that they were loved, so they followed their heart (injured and sinful as it was). The deal of a lifetime was presented, and they swallowed the bait—hook, line and sinker. Even if they had been told in advance, they probably would not have turned from their ways. Why? Pride carried them miles further than they wanted to go. You see, people are funny creatures. They will do anything to feel important and accepted. In the garden, Satan drew them as close to his way of thinking by the friendliness that he presented as he did by the temptation itself. That's why gang membership works. The people on the outside have no one, and so they want on the inside so they can belong. They would rather chance the wrath of the law enforcement than to have no one care. That's why the gothic lifestyle works. That is way the gypsy lifestyle works. That's why the bar scene works. That's why the technological age is working. People want to stay connected.

Froggie knew something was up on this particular day. Different men had been tasked to look in his cage all day long, sometimes in groups and sometimes with extra food. At first, Froggie thought that maybe it was his day of promotion—the day he would receive his crown. But reality said that they were at a lot of other frogs' pens, and notes were compared. Who was the strongest, and who was the fastest? Who had jumped out of the hot water quicker? Who had been there the longest? It didn't seem to matter to Froggie anymore. He was tired of the cage, he was tired of the loneliness, he was even tired of trying to think that he was someone. Let the man have his way no matter what. Hope was dying in his heart that day, and so was the desire to be someone.

We may not want to face the day with all that is troubling our world, but, dear ones, face it we must. We are not hopeless, and we are someone very important. We are children of the King. We are *sons* and *daughters* of the Father of all mankind. I do believe what I have written, and the very reason that it is called the Internet is that we are being drawn in to our demise. It is the exact reason it is call the World Wide Web. We get stuck to it, and then the nasty ole spider comes along and wraps us up and then sucks the life out of us. Before you know it, we can do anything but follow along. No, you don't have to believe me. Yes, you can call me names if you like. Of course, you don't have to agree with what has been stated, because everything is going to turn around and I will be proven a false prophet. But as I have stated at the beginning of this book, if I'm wrong, oh, well. If I'm right, you and I had better get ready for what is to come. Listen to Matthew for a minute: "Watch out that no one deceives you. For any will come in my name, claiming, 'I am the Christ,' and will deceive many" (Matt. 24:4–5).

There has never been a time in history that so many have come forward and claimed to be the Christ. There has never been a time when so many have fallen for the lies of the devil in following false religions. We stay huddled in our little churches and pretend that there is nothing happening out there. It is happening, and the church has had its head stuck in the sand. "You will hear of wars and rumors of wars, but see to it that you are not alarmed" (Matt. 24:6).

We have always had wars around the world. Several have included the whole world. But we have never had such a time as this. It's broadcast throughout the whole world each war and all the propaganda that goes along with it. Right now, after trying to clean up the Middle East, more internal wars are starting each day. The young people seem to be some of the perpetrators. Guess who have been on the computer more than anyone else. Guess who is primed to fall in line. *Revolt* seems to be the word of the day like no other day. "There will be famines and earthquakes in various places" (Matt. 24:8).

We have to be blind to not see what has been happening to our world. The evening news sets the stage for this verse to be true. Earthquakes are at an all-time high. They, in turn, cause thing to happen to the earth so that other natural disasters take place. Millions and millions of people are starving because of those disasters. We, in America, sit back and throw crumbs to the rest of the world, thinking we have done something great, thinking that the real devastation won't come near us. I know this to be true because we are continuing to believe that we can curb the tide and America will return to the way it was.

Our greed has blinded us to the world takeover. We have a president we don't agree with because of his spending habits. We don't like him because he took away the National Day of Prayer and gave it to the Muslims. We are upset that he has changed our health care and slipped it in when no one was looking. Folks, *wake up!* He did these things on national TV. He hasn't been afraid to let the people know exactly what he has been doing. In fact, he has been on TV more than any president has ever been. The State of the Nation Address has been seen in increments every other day, if not every day. The leapfrog effect has escalated to a new level. The last shocking thing has just happened, and another comes along until we are not only forgetting the last shocking thing but confused about what is really taking place. Then we are zoomed to a new national disaster and then to another war that has started. There is no hope and doesn't seem to be any help in sight. Give up? Give in?

Who is this man with all the answers? Who is this who can straighten out so many situations at one time? Who is this who can organize so many people with such precision? Who is this man who can get everyone's attention? Our president only asked us if we wanted change. He was a shoo-in because we wanted change. The tool has done a good job in preparing the populace to accept change. Has change been good or bad? Pull your head out of the sand, and take a look.

Froggie was in one of those moods today. He willingly jumped into the frying pan; I mean, the man's hands. He had resolved that he might as well live out the day and not buck the system anymore. After all, what could they do to him? It wasn't as if it were a matter of life and death. It wasn't like he could turn back or anything. At least there is food.

> Poor Froggie. He just won't listen. He wouldn't listen to his mom and pop, his best friend, or his own heart.
>
> Well, all the way down the hall, past all the other cages, he could see the eyes of all his friends peering out at him. They looked so sad and seemed to look all the way into his heart and see his sadness. It was when he was carried by Frogette's cage… The panic that filled her face was almost more than he could take. He wanted to holler out to her that he would see her tomorrow, but the words locked up in his throat. He wondered in his mind if this was the day of his doom. Was this the day that he would be plunged into the boiling water to his death? He fought to get a grip on his mind so that he wouldn't go crazy with fear. He had to trust the man…with his life…didn't he?

Fear blinds the world into believing the lie so much so that we become paralyzed. We know that we are doomed, and yet…we do nothing to save ourselves. We look into the eyes of other's, and we see their sadness... They see ours. We do nothing. "As it was in the days of Noah, so it will be with the coming of the Son of man." We put our trust in the economy even though we see it collapsing. We put our trust in medicine even though we don't get any better. We put our trust in man, and we know that he has an evil intent. Then we turn around and complain that God has abandoned us in our time of need. Yet we have trusted in everything and everyone but him. There is no peace within.

We watch the evening news, we read the newspaper, and we listen to the politician all with an expectancy that the answer will soon be coming. Our kids are going further and further away from us, so we psychoanalyze them. We teach them new things to keep their interest...how to waste your time with fifty different ways of... using the computer. No, you say. Why then are so many going off the deep end? Why are so many getting so rebellious? Why are they on so many drugs? We are leapfrogging them into the fire, and because of our pride, we will not stop teaching them...what to do wrong. We look at the gifted and say, "Let them teach our children." We fail to see; no, we fail to acknowledge that those same people have gods other than the one whom we are supposed to be following—gods of money, good looks, position, and power. Because they look good, because they have good pedigrees, we say that they are the ones to teach our children.

Let me clarify. We would never let a murderer teach our children. Sorry, Paul, you are out. We would never let a prostitute teach our children. Sorry, Mary, you're out. We would never let one who had been demon possessed teach our children. Sorry, man from the Gerasenes, you're out. At least, they would not be our first pick or second or third or fourth...

We would choose the ones who are somebody we can trust, somebody who thinks like we do, somebody who is a yes-man to the age that we live in, who will fall in line with what everybody else is doing because "they" say it is right. Sorry, Elijah, you're out. You were always telling someone that they were doing wrong. Sorry, Jesus, you're out. Why is Jesus out? Because he bucked the system all the way. He turned the tables on them. He exposed their greed, infested hearts, and slick deceptive ways that they used to control men. They cried out that they were right and that he was wrong. They cried out until they had crucified the Savior of the world...for doing good.

I have seen it outside the church and inside the church. It makes no difference. But what gets to my very soul is the fact that we don't accept any of the blame for why things are the way they are. Yet we ourselves mimic the rich and famous and their road to success. We turn the church into a business and copy the patterns for good business practices. We forget that Peter was told to throw his nets on the other side of the boat—great success; take his rod, reel down to the seashore, and catch the first fish; and then take the coin out of its mouth and pay the temple tax—great success. We forget that the disciples were to pass out a sack lunch and feed fifteen thousand people... Great success! You say, five thousand men, get your story straight. I say five thousand men plus women and children. You see, when you begin to turn the church into a business, you begin to lose sight of God. And when you lose sight of God, you begin to follow man. And when you begin to follow man, you begin to lose your life because of man's choices. That, my friend, is what happened in the garden. The cost was way greater than mankind's wildest dreams.

Now you think that because we are so advanced and we are so able that everything is going so well... We are closer than ever before to the Second Coming of Christ. To control the world and to get the people to follow there is going to have to be an instrument that will lead the people to their own destruction. My friend, man following man, eating from the tree of good and evil, using an instrument that is beginning to control the people, and making everything that we do and say revolve around the computer. So, so blind, so, so thickheaded, so, so much falling into bondage...with our eyes wide open...with our ears so closed...with our hearts so full of pride... with our minds so clouded with earthly thoughts.

Froggie was sure glad that the man eased him into the water that day. He just wasn't sure that he could take the plunge, so to speak. At least, the water was tolerable, and it was not like the day the man flopped him into the hot water. It might be a good day after all. He lay there, swam a little, and zapped a fly now and then. Ohhh, this is starting to feel so good, and the desire to just float became more than tempting… It became a reality. Now he did notice that the man kept coming back and turning the heat up little by little. But it sure did feel good. All those arthritic joints…all those bad thoughts… all those fears…

I just applied for Social Security. Guess what. I heard that I can have it directly deposited, or I can receive a debit card. I haven't received notice yet, but the source was pretty reliable. Cashless society? Can't buy or sell without the mark? Your card just got stolen, and we want to put a mark on your right hand or your forehead. It sickens me that one of these days I will have to make the ultimate decision. It's not that far-off either. Where will my allegiants be placed? Whom will I trust? Will I be able to make the decision unto death? Read this passage from Revelations 12: "They overcame him, by the blood of the Lamb and by the word of their testimony; they did not love their lives so much as to shrink from death."

I don't know exactly when it happened, but Froggie's mind got real foggie. The water had gotten so hot that he couldn't move at all anymore. He started to dream of the pond back home and all the fun that he had when he was growing up, and he remembered sitting around, eating, and reminiscing with the family about all the trouble that he had caused when did his own thing. Well, at least this time they all laughed with him. Good dreams, good times, good friends…and then his heart began to feel so funnyyy.

Froggie's heart had just quit. Boiled to death in his own "dream" pond at the hands of the man who had promised to take care of him. Why didn't he jump out of the pond like he did before when it was so hot? Well, let's just say that Froggie had gotten so comfortable with what he had planned, that he didn't see that the man had another plan that eventually led to his destruction. Let's say that it is a very sad thing that *poor* Froggie hadn't listened...

World War 2 was hot water, boiling hot water. It took a while for the Americans to realize that we were going to be boiled to death if we let Hitler continue with his rampage and desire for world take-over. When we came to our senses, we jumped from the pond of boiling water to our safety. Our skin was red and blistered, but at least we were alive. Now this go-round; we just don't get the fact that the only world power to be contended with will not be bullied into submission. We will fight back with all our might. We don't get the fact that to conquer a nation like ours, something has to be done that will bring us to our knees.

Pride cometh before the fall.

To get the opponent to fall, you must appeal to his pride. He then will think more of himself than he should. It gets him into position for the fall. Let me ask you a straightforward question. Do you think that the USA has been set up to be proud of what it has achieved and become—more medals in the Olympic games, the greatest army in the world, first to the moon, more millionaires, more "football, baseball, hockey, basketball" pride at every level? And this is for every red-blooded American who has any sense of value. We have subdivisions full of houses that are two and three stories tall and with elaborate furnishing for a family of two, three, or four people that show the world just how rich and cultured we are. The list goes on and on concerning our pride that sets us up for the fall.

Now don't forget, friend, that's what God's Word says, not what I say. In the church, that's why we give out medals or recognition for the biggest church, the fastest-growing church, and the most innovative church with the best programs. In the church, that is why we raise the "greatest" men to the greatest pastorates. That man has the gift. It doesn't matter if he has humility. It doesn't matter if he has a love that reaches into the dirt for fallen mankind. It doesn't matter if he is more concerned about supporting his program with your money than supporting the littlest church that can hardly make a go of it. He is the man…to brag about. Okay, excuse yourself, and pretend that what I'm saying is a lie. But look on the paper and see whom you just chose. Look for a minute whom you gave acclaim to. It wasn't Joe Smoe from Timbuktu. It was your glamorous, well-educated, pedigreed prince from the long line of princes. Too bad, disciples, you wouldn't be chosen in this century by the men who "run" the church today. You're not smart enough. Your family heritage isn't good enough. It's just a good thing that we finally have improved on what God started so long ago. We are so proud of who we are and have become!

> But God chose the foolish things of the world to shame the wise; God chose the weak things of the world to shame the strong. He chose the lowly things of this world and the despised things—and the things that are not—to nullify the things that are, so that no one may boast before him. (1 Cor. 1:27)

Did your church give a good offering last week (for the Lord, of course)? The widow gave enough to get Jesus's attention so that he would say, "Now that's what I call an offering." Did you just build a great building and call it *church*? Jesus told those who would listen that the story of the lady who just washed his feet with her hair would be told to everyone for all generations. You know what? It is still being told. God hasn't changed his plan…but we have, and we're boasting about. We are setting ourselves up for the fall.

Get a house divided, and it will fall.

Oldest trick in the book, but we still fall for it. Our nation, if you will take time to notice, is very divided against itself. What we haven't noticed is that it has been intentional. There has been a planned attack between those who are good Christian people and those who are not Christians and are not good people. The news purposely shows the tea party's efforts in light of the government's plan to put this bill into place for the common good of the people. Naturally, everyone thinks that the issue is money because both sides serve money as a minigod. The issue, if you will take note, is dividing the country. Split it down the middle, and the fall will be sure to take place. It matters not about the economics. That will always be brought to the forefront, but it is not the issue. Teachers against the system, for money, ballplayers against the powers to be and it's all about money. The government doing things that irritate all of us. Notice it's all about money. Notice all these issues that cause friction are about money. All hail King Money. *Poof* and division has taken place.

Ask yourself, what is one of the definite issues that cause marital conflicts? Have a church board meeting. What causes the most contention? What part of the government don't you like? It wouldn't happen to be the fact that they shaved off some of your money, now, is it? When you last agued with your spouse, was it about money she wanted to spend and you did not?

To get the house divided, you have to use their god. To use their god, you have to cause them to argue about proper use of that particular god. Don't give me that nonsense. You know it's true. It isn't just about money. It can be anything that we demand to be the reason for our happiness. Maybe that is why we don't have to argue about whether or not Christianity is right. Maybe that is why we argue so much. We're not happy.

Make the world you live in very impersonal.

If it is the sweatbox used as a torture device or for solitary confinement helped to control people, then the computer will continue to be used to control people. Outside the box or on the other side of the bars, the effect is the same. Those who watch the process see that there is punishment for those who do wrong. Fear sets in, and care is given so as not to get caught looking at something you should not be looking at or talking to someone whom you should not be talking to, or even wasting time that should not be wasted.

We talk around the world but won't talk to our spouse. We look into the world of imagination but won't study the Bible, because we can't see God. We buy stuff that we don't need and fail to go out of the house, because we can order online. We are shy in person because we know they can see the red creeping into our face when we are embarrassed. We won't go to church, because we don't like crowds. I am positive that you can shoot down every one of my examples, "Oh no, I don't." That's because you're only thinking of yourself. You won't take time to look honestly at society and their true nature. You will tell me to look at the football stadium and ask if more people aren't going there in large crowds. Yes, but is it not to see one of the gods of this age? Isn't it to go and cheer about something that does not matter at all? Isn't it to kill the pain in broken homes and the messed-up country that we live in?

Deny it if you like. But while you're at it, deny Columbine. While you're at it, deny all the suicides that take place daily. While you're at it, deny all the divorces that take place for the third or fourth times in people's lives. Deny the many abortions that separate young women from the life they were intended to live. Somebody got lonely, and somebody got left out, and we are now in trouble because it is becoming the norm, and we can't see the foothold it has gained in our society. The fire goes out, and the strength leaves, and there is nothing left to fight with except conjured-up notions about what should be. The fall is inevitable when people are separated and lonely.

Cause people to think less of God and his Son,
cause them to forget his Holy Spirit

We think less of God in two ways. He is not who he says he is, and we use less time to think about God. The first is happening with a planned effort to get you to think that God isn't who you say he is. A chip here and a chip there, and slowly the resolve to stand up for who God really is, is taken away. Take away prayer from school so that you can respect other's rights. Bingo, you have reduced God to being second-class. Take the Ten Commandments off the wall of the courtroom because it offends the people that break those laws. Bingo, you have reduced his Word to being not important. Tell the Christian that he cannot talk about the Lord in public areas (schools and such). Bingo, you have taken away God's voice. Take "In God we trust" off our money, and bingo, you have taken away the presence of God. No, silly, you can take away God and his ability in any of these areas. But the push is happening so that a technological age of young people will think less of the God who created all things and died on a cross for our sins and came back in the form of the Holy Spirit to lead us into all truths.

Secondly, there is another push to get us to think less time about God. There is an argument going around as to when the Sabbath day is. I don't have time to argue. I do know that after many years of studying church attendance, I have found that large corporations have gotten into the habit of making sure that all people have to work on Sunday at one time or another. I don't know why they have to do that, but it is true. It seems to be said, "Separate them from the Word of God."

People in general are so much busier than they were in the past. Making money, playing sports, and going here and there so they can get peace and rest are only a few ways that the Word of God is kept from the populace. After an early rise to get to work to make money, they march on toward the wind-down time after work. Playing at this and that, they find that there is not really any time soon that they can play with God (as if he were a toy). Next, off to the kids or the grandkids and friends and neighbors in the name of our Savior (you have to love them, don't you?). It is forgotten that we will miss the spoken Word of God with so many places to go. In fact, in today's age, a good series of messages can't be given because not enough people are there for the duration of the series. It's sort of like point *A*...

point *D*… Pastor, how do those fit together? I don't get it. No you don't, not really.

You forget God and the fall will come quicker than you think.

Get people to quit praying, and the fall will come.

There are two types of prayer that we forget: believing prayer and time-consuming prayer. Let's go to the second, first. Have you ever left your wife or husband a note like "I'm going here or there and will be right back"? Then you add at the end of the note, "I love you"? Face it, leaving that little touch, over the long run, will not get it. They will, at some time, need to spend more time with you so that they will know that you mean it. And besides, if you really do love someone, you're going to want to spend time with them, a lot of time. Why, because you enjoy their company. Now company isn't sitting there watching TV or being in the same room while you read a book. Company is talking over the day, making plans, and saying, "I care about who we are together." God is no different. We must take time with him, and that time has to be in recognition that he is present. To do that will take time. You give your time to everything else, don't you?

The first area concerns believing prayer. "Now I lay me…," "God is good," "God is great," "Thank you for this food…" are not the type of believing prayer that I'm talking about. I am not talking about the type of prayer that centers on the family and is a repetition of the prayer from the day before or even bless our church service today. "Believing" prayer first recognizes the immensity of the being of God, how real he is, how present he is, how powerful he is, how knowing he is, and how *holy* he is. If we did believe that our lives would change drastically, we wouldn't talk as if we knew so much about God and the plan he has for our lives. We probably wouldn't be as flippant when talking about him. He can see everything that's done, he can hear every word that is spoken, he knows every thought that is thought, he will not be intimidated by anyone, he will never be beaten into submission, he knows what to do in every situation, his plans never fail, he's never lost a child who has trusted in him, he has enough provision for any need, and for sure, he is sovereign.

Friend, if we really believed that, our prayer lives would change. If only we could see that there is nothing that is impossible for the one we call God, who would then be our enemy that would control us or make us fear or cause us all this anxiety? The fall will come when we quit praying believing, time-consuming prayers.

Get people to no longer take God's Word seriously.

One item that has helped me in so many ways down through time is the memorization of scripture. Somehow, it gets beneath the surface of my mind and begins to have meaning to me. When I get faced with it day after day until I memorized it, God will show me the reason that the verse or verses are so important to me. He will also show me what the conditions of the promises are so I can have the full benefit of what his Word has said to me.

People, on the other hand, give every excuse in the book as to why they can't memorize scripture. I just don't have that gift anymore. I don't have the time it would take to keep scripture before me. Could it be possible that there are other reasons we can't memorize scripture? Take for instance, why do men know all the players of many of the sports teams as well as the scores and status and batting averages? Why do you think that women are able to know so many things like sowing, gardening, cooking, what happened on the TV soap the day (weeks and months) before, who wore what last Sunday, or all the wrongs a husband did? Could it be because they memorized what was important to them. You go to work, and they lay out the tasks before you. It wouldn't be good advice to say, "Forget what they told you." You memorize it so you can do your job well and get that coveted raise that you desired. And yet, here we are, handling the greatest news ever to come down the line, and we can't put it to memory. That's all memorization is—putting into our mind something to be remembered, something important, something that will affect our lives forever.

We also handle the truth with a buffet-type attitude. If I like what it says and it will benefit me, I'll take it. If it doesn't benefit me, *forget* it.

We mishandle scripture by turning the meaning so that it will serve us. Two little illustrations:

1. First Corinthians 10:13b makes the statement that "And God is faithful; he will not let you be tempted beyond what you can bear." Man's translation has two parts to the translation. First, he forgets that the scripture is talking about being tempted to sin. And secondly, he looks at the words "how much you can bear," which means how much pressure or how many trials you can handle. His rendition comes across like this: *God will not give us any more than we can handle.*

Now it no longer talks about sin, the real subject matter, just our comfort and support. It appeals to the multitude, and the gospel is perverted. And listen, folks, it's not just the common folks who translate it that way. It's the whole of the American people—including professors, pastors, and teachers—who misquote this verse this way. We aren't called to carry anything. "Come unto me, you who labor and are heavy burdened and I will give you rest." We are called to be done with sin, "for the wages of sin is death."

When the scripture is treated in this way, sheer disaster is on the way. That's why even Christian people commit suicide. The verse has failed them.

2. Romans 8:28 states that all things work for the good... Why did I trail there? Because that is where every red-blooded human being stops (many do). They want something good to happen to them, so they try to picture God doing something good for them. First of all, that is very self-centered. Secondly, it forgets, again, that there are conditions and goals set in the other scriptures that surround that particular verse. Before, it talks about allowing the Holy Spirit to pray through us because we don't know what we ought to pray. All things take us to the point that we recognize the fact that we don't know what to pray. The

verses after talk about being made into the image of the firstborn Son, Jesus. All things, good and bad, take us to the point where we will know that unless God does the work within us, we will never become Christlike. People's translation: God works in all things for *my* good (not his good), so I can now be thankful for the good things that happen to me but not the bad things. The bad things hurt too much to be thankful for.

You just think I don't know what I'm talking about. I listen to people…a lot—professors, pastors, teachers, as well as the common folks. They all translate it the same, and the end result is God's Word being mishandled. We fail to see that this will set us up for the fall because our hopes will be dashed by the wayside when God's Word seems to fail us, when we become mindless, and when we don't know how to pray, because we have run out of words. His purpose is the key words to Romans 8:28.

Well, Froggie died a fruitless death. His goals and aspirations vanished even though he was a fictional character. It's true that a frog will jump from a pan of hot water but will lie there and die when the water is heated in slow increments. It is also true that if threatened, the human will come out fighting, but when given piecemeal lies, he will fall hook, line and sinker into his own demise. You still aren't convinced that the computer is the instrument that will be used for the great delusion. But take time to check out Revelations 13:11–17:

> Then I saw another beast, coming out of the earth. He had two horns like a lamb, but he spoke like a dragon. He exercised all the authority of the first beast on his behalf, and made the earth and its inhabitants worship the first beast, whose fatal wound had been healed. And he performed great and miraculous signs, even causing fire to come down from heaven to earth in full view of men. Because of the signs he was given power to do on behalf of the first beast,

he deceived the inhabitants of the earth. He ordered them to set up an image in honor of the beast who was wounded by the sword and yet lived. He was given power to give breath to the image of the first beast, so that it could speak and cause all who refuse to worship the image to be killed. He also forced everyone, small and great, rich and poor, free and slave, to receive a mark on his right hand or on his forehead, so that no one could buy or sell unless he had the mark, which is the name of the beast or the number of his name.

When you look at the fact that there will be an image of the beast, don't you get the foggiest idea that perhaps it is a computer that is built to look like the beast, programmed with such technology that it will appear to be alive? Can't you take the time to couple that with the grocery store and the scan lines that don't need a person but use a computer? Can't you couple that with the fact that no one will be able to buy or sell with a mark? Why is it that you are still so hung up on proving me wrong that you can't see the wizardry of lulling our minds to sleep so that we accept this lie that Satan has told. Witchcraft cast spells over others so that those others can do the bidding of the "witch." Tell me truthfully. In our last election, did the nation get a spell cast upon it so that the election turned out the way Satan wanted it to turn out? We are not better because we chose someone that promised change (the promise was for good). We are not less in debt than before the election. It's doubled and maybe even tripled. Rich men were given money that they neither deserved nor needed. Poor men are now taxed more heavily than before. Christianity is going down the tubes faster than any time in history. We are being boiled to death, and we aren't doing a thing about getting ourselves ready for that death. Yes, I said we are going to die, our country, our way of doing things, our ability to resist, our way of worship, and even our very lives. We are going to die. You will holler, "Foul." What a negative attitude. Read

Jeremiah. He could see the handwriting on the wall. Read Ezekiel. He heard from God and proclaimed what was to come. No, dah! I'm not either of those two. Nevertheless, the handwriting is on the wall. The fall is inevitable. Go ahead and read back though the points that lead to the fall and deny that it is coming. Deceive yourself so that you don't have to have a nervous breakdown when faced with what is coming. Lie to your children and grandchildren by telling them that everything will be okay as they progress into the future. Let them get more and more hypnotized as they play their computer games. Get them the newest and the latest technology so they can enter into the "new age" with the ability to change their world. I have feeling that they will be part of the changes that are going to be made.

But there is one thing that I hope you don't do. Don't you dare forget that I told you what is going to take place in the future of this country and our world. Don't you dare forget that I warned you to get yourself ready for the upcoming holocaust that is going to descend upon us with vengeance. Don't forget that neither God nor I want anyone to be lulled to sleep in an eternal death, like Froggie was. Don't forget:

> Then He said to them all: "If anyone would come after me, he must deny himself and take up his cross daily and follow me. For whoever wants to save his life will lose it, but whoever loses his life for me will save it. What good is it for a man to gain the whole world, and yet lose or forfeit his very self." (Luke 9:23–25)

You don't have anything on this earth worth keeping compared to what we will gain over there. It is my desire to help you see some of the things that will help us to get ready. The answer is Jesus Christ as Savior and the Holy Spirit as the guide. The Father has done everything and given everything to get us to heaven. May we not perish because we failed to receive what he has offered.

What to Do? What to Do? Oh My, What to Do?

It wouldn't be proper to talk about what is to come and not give thoughts as to what will help us find our way through the computer age, the very tool that will lead many astray. This isn't a how-to but a must, so please treat it as if your very life depended on the outcome. Froggie's predicament is our predicament. The difference is our eternal destiny. Jesus did not die for frogs, but he did die for you and me. Jesus was plunged into the hottest water and didn't jump back out. It wasn't someone else's idea; it was his Father's. You will have to ask yourself one question. Whose hot water do you want to end up in when it all goes down? The hot water of the world because you refuse to go their way, or the hot water many will be in because they failed to follow God? One gives way to eternal death, and one leads to eternal life. Your choice, my friend.

Pride

Froggie's downfall started with his pride that was built on the compliments of others and probably his progress because he was an exceptional frog. He won a few races and a few medals, and maybe he was given an important tidal. His parents probably thought nothing of it at the time because according to the psychology reports it was good for his self-esteem. Besides, they were still trying to get him to overcome his complex of having no legs when he was born. Maybe he had a wart on his nose or his spots didn't turn as green as they should have, or perhaps his dad had been king of the pond at one time. No matter, the fact is Froggie's pride got the best of him, and it got him in a lot of hot water.

Why does pride get the best of us, and how do we overcome it? First off, you have to recognize pride for what it is, the very enemy of our soul. Everything that comes against us is nothing compared to pride.

It took Satan down and many angels with him, and I don't understand why we should follow in his footsteps, but we do. The beginning of Satan's downfall was the same as Froggie's. Someone told him that he was something that he was not. Maybe it was his own mind; or maybe it was one of the other angels who wanted to be like him—handsome, wise, and powerful, to name a few. He was built by God to be all those things and so much more that words can't describe. But Satan was never destined to be God. He was not the one to call the shots. He was not the one to call things into existence. He was not the one that everyone should look to for answers. But maybe, just maybe, one of the lesser angels looked upon him with a little too much adoration. I don't really know. I do know that pride starts somewhere.

It's sort of like the young boy at church camp. He was the best-looking kid there and had more athletic ability in his little finger than I have had in a lifetime. Smart...as a whip! I played God that day and would interview each of the kids and end with telling them whether or not they could come into heaven. This dear little fellow thought it best to argue with God when I told him that he couldn't come in. "What have I done wrong? Where don't I measure up? I've dotted all my *i*'s and crossed all my *t*'s. I'm great at Bible quizzing, and I attend church every Sunday with my parents. I take out the garbage when told. I'm a straight A student." Yes, friend, he was a model for humanity. In fact, I would have chosen him to stand beside me anywhere. He was that type of kid. Ya just had to love him. The problem was, Junior never gave me the only reason that he should be allowed in heaven. He never told me that he was a filthy rotten sinner and that he needed Jesus's saving grace, or he wouldn't make it in. He just told me all his good qualities and thought they would be sure to get him in. That was the basis of his argument. That argument was built on sifting sand, not the solid rock. His pride, like Froggie's, would be his demise.

If ever you're going to make it to God's eternal abode, you also will have to give the reason that God should let you in. No advanced technology will ever come close to getting you there. But I know that it might keep you from getting there. Look at it this way. Anytime I have defended myself, I have found that it was my pride that had been insulted, and I wanted that point rectified. Therefore, I set myself on a course that justified me. Jesus is the only one that justifies. We don't need to defend ourselves. He is our defense attorney.

Now we will get down to where the rubber meets the road. Why would you defend the computer or technology so adamantly? Why does it anger you that one as insignificant as me would speak against the computer age when it is so full of progress? Perhaps the pride of accomplishment and ease? Could it be that you don't believe one who does so much for you would lead you astray, or maybe you think me the fool and tell yourself that Jesus will keep you from getting "caught" by the net? Your pride will be your down fall in the end.

> Do not love the world or anything in the world. If anyone loves the world, the love of the Father is not in him. For everything in the world—the cravings of the sinful man, the lust of his eyes, and the boasting of what he has and does—comes not from the Father but from the world. The world and its desires pass away, but the man who does the will of God lives for ever. (1 John 2:15–17)

Paul stated that all his righteousness was as filthy rags. He counted them as dung. We, on the other hand, think because of all our big buildings and accomplishments that we are in like Flynn with God. Peter wept when faced with his failures of confessing Christ. The only thing that makes some of us cry is our loss or our failure in itself.

We are so prideful when it comes to who we are, and we seem to look down our nose at others who don't measure up to our standards. They don't dress as good as we do, they don't have the degrees that we do, they don't have the size bank accounts as we do, they don't own as much as we do, they can't speak as well as we do, they can't structure things as well as we can structure them…and we don't let them lead because we are better than they are… Praise God. It doesn't matter that they have childlike faith, they have humility beyond degree, or they love others in such a way that others flock to them for help.

Joseph came to our VBS, and because he was just a little mentally challenged, I let him get on the bus. As it turned out, he wanted to help with the children at recess. In today's world, the red flags shot up everywhere. Oh no, what if we haven't had him checked out yet...? Yada, yada, yada... Yet in my spirit, the God of the universe told me to let him help. Yes, I had to overcome my fears, but what was that compared to helping someone who had been rejected for years come to know how much Jesus (and us) loved him? The only thing that Joseph could do because of his size (extra-extra-extralarge) was belly buck the children as they ran at him wide open. He was the "hit" of the Bible school. Kids couldn't wait to get to recess, nor could he.

To complete his story, we and his whole family got to be good friends and still are today. He never could read well, but did he know his Bible? He instructed some of the dear folks as to the right and the wrong of different situations, and that included yours truly. He cared for the folks who came to the church who sometimes didn't fit in. And yet...for all the care that he had in his big heart, he was looked down on by those who were rich in the things of the world. He was a second-class Christian to them but not to Jesus. Who had the pride? Who was following Jesus? Who would you choose to live beside in heaven? For that matter, who would get to heaven? Don't judge either. Pray for both.

So what do I do to get past the tool that may lead me to a trap that is being set for me and mine? What do I do to skirt around the plan that is so deceptive that even the very elect could be deceived? Humble yourself. Admit that you are not God and that the plan to deceive you is bigger than you are and that you can't find your way with technology. Admit that the tree of the knowledge of good and evil is going to be harmful to you and yours unless extreme caution is used. Admit that you can't walk hand in hand with those who are not of the family of God. Admit that you will pull in two different directions. Admit that if left to yourself, you are sinfully disposed to serving created things including yourself. Admit that you have deep within your heart a desire to fit in rather than swim upstream. Admit that pride cometh before the fall.

> If my people, who are called by my name,
> will humble themselves and pray and seek my
> face and turn from their wicked ways, then will
> I hear from heaven and will forgive their sin and
> will heal their land. Now my eyes will be open
> and my ears attentive to the prayers offered in
> this place. (2 Chronicles 7:14)

Call, humble, pray, seek, and turn from... Need I say more?

Unity

Froggie always seemed to think about *his* success and *his* goals and *his* position in life. Everybody else was on the back burner. Denomination after denomination has been created because of a difference of opinion. Church after church has been created because of difference of opinion. Church after church has likeminded people who fit with the décor, financial status, and cultural demeanor; and everybody else is excluded. My son was asked to start a church but, when confronted with a certain question, had to decline. Who are we going to minister to? What age group and what economic status? Jesus died that we might all get saved. Jesus died that we might be brought into unity like the Son had with the Father. No exclusions and no exceptions were prayed for when Jesus went to the garden before he went to the cross. I was at a church that wanted revival but didn't want Blacks to come as a part of the morning worship. What is wrong with that picture? We are all going to be in heaven together. What are we going to say to Jesus? "Could you put those who aren't like us over there or down below? Could you keep the Blacks from coming *up* to our street?" Don't you see why the fall could come so quickly? Don't you see why we could be led away so easily? Prejudice is sin, folks, because it is full of pride; and as long as there is sin in our life, we can be led astray.

Unity is all looking to Christ, and Christ does not lead people to be separated from each other. Paul disagreed about taking Mark with them on a missionary journey, so Barnabas took him along with him. But guess what. Later, Paul asks for Mark to come to him because of his helpfulness to his ministry. God led him back into unity within the body. Too bad when things go wrong, we can't be led back into unity. We don't even try. We separate from those who didn't agree with us and start another church. We get mad because they didn't choose the color that we like, and so we quit tithing. They didn't choose us to sing the solo, so we quit the choir. We say, "If they continue to come here, then I quit." You say that I don't know what I'm talking about…but deep in your heart, you know I am speaking the truth.

Unity is something to behold when acted out with Christ at the head instead of the tail. Philippians 2 talks about Christ becoming humble in his attitude so that we could get saved as he went to the cross. Listen to the ifs of this chapter.

> If you have any encouragement from being united with Christ, if any comfort from his love, if any tenderness and compassion, then make my joy complete by being like-minded, having the same love, being one in spirit and purpose. Do nothing out of selfish ambition or vain conceit, but in humility consider other "better" than yourselves. Each of you should look not to your own interests, but also to the interests of others. (Phil. 2:1–4)

"If" you don't have any encouragement, comfort, tenderness, and compassion, I'm thinking that maybe you have missed the Christ that I serve. But also listen to what happens "if" these things happen to you. You will consider others in the equation every time. How can I help them succeed? What can I do so that they are included in the program of glorifying God? Because if we look closely, we will see that all decisions to be made for the kingdom can be reduced down to two factors. Will the outcome of this decision glorify God, and will it cause the people to come together? It will not be an individual decision made because of a personal preference where someone's genius will be heralded.

How does this play out in the computer world? There seems to be a division between the generations. One generation that has learned many things from hardships of living and war, to the next generation that lives at such a fast pace. The two are being separated, and whether we want to admit it or not, it is causing friction. The younger wants new technology and gadgets that promote the worship service, and the older wants to stay in the past where it is slow enough to keep pace with.

One group wants music that is fast pace and tuned to the ear of this age, and the other group wants to tune into a more traditional song that we are used to hearing. I can hear your thoughts now. "I don't want to go back to the ole pond where all the mold and mildew are." What I can also hear is that you are not saying anything about the division that has been created and the fact that the church is being torn apart just because of individual preference. I can hear rumblings within the heart that say. "I'm right, and you're wrong." Who cares who's right? Is there any worship going on when we argue? Is he really included or considered as to his preference?

The new gimmick syndrome and the instant sight system that is being put into place by the computer is at fault for leading people into following their feelings and calling it the Holy Spirit. You do know that you can get a rush of adrenaline when playing computer games, don't you? Isn't it funny that you can't see how that is brought into the church service every week? Exciting…spirit filled? If you don't get it, don't worry; neither do the older people. They just think that the younger people hate them and are trying to make their lives miserable.

How do I remove the barrier that Satan is trying to place in front of me with computer technology? Let the Holy Spirit begin to control all your decisions with *others in mind*. Teach each other what it is to let *someone else's decision be important*. Realize that there is a plan that is being inserted into this generation of time that is going to divide them. Then *pray until* God shows you how to fix the problem. Don't give way to division! If this subject was so important when

Jesus went to the garden, it is that much more important today. He prayed for unity and love (John 17), the two subjects that matter to God; and we should be praying for that to happen today. He didn't pray for the colors of the carpet to end up to my liking; he prayed for unity. He didn't pray for what type of music to sing on Sunday morning; he prayed for unity. He didn't pray for what type of people should come to our church; he prayed for unity.

It's a personal Gospel.

Have you ever talked with someone who would not give you a chance to speak? Sure you have. You knew that you would have to be rude or walk away to end the conversation. This is become more evident as time goes on. I talked to a pastor acquaintance the other day and experienced this to the ultimate. He found a subject that sparked his mind and never slowed down the whole time I was with him. I even tried to interrupt him. Finally, I said to him, "You can't hear me, can you?" It didn't faze him in the least. I had to tell him goodbye and just walk away because he wouldn't shut up.

Maybe I was the one who was rude, but in today's age, this is becoming a big problem. As I sought for answers of why this was taking place, I came across at least one of the answers. You're going to grow, but here goes anyway. The computer has created a society that can talk and talk and talk without stopping, and they can say whatever they want as many times as they want to whomever they want until they are blue in the face as many times as they want to get blue in the face day or night, night or day no matter what the time of day is, and they can use as many words as they want, and you can't stop them even if you wanted to, because they are in charge of the keyboard or the keypad, so you know what I am talking about... Wow, I almost ran out of breath after that little sentence. But it is true. The communication system that has been installed into our lives leaves little room to listen to each other.

First, we don't listen to each other's hearts. Over the Internet or on the computer phone (texting), we can't hear the passion, sorrow, or intent of the heart. We can say mean things that aren't really an expression of what is going on in our lives. We prattle on and on about stuff that really doesn't matter or shouldn't be said.

Secondly, we switch from one person to another faster than a speeding bullet, short bursts that last only a few seconds. This falls in line with everything else in our lives that chop up our attention span. We can't focus long enough to get deep into the subject.

God's Word tells us to be slow to speak and quick to listen. The computer age has taught us just the opposite, quick to speak and slow to listen. That's true because you can come back hours later to listen to the heart of someone who needed to talk right now but you were busy texting someone else. Remember, today's generation and the plan, not just your own little world that you think so much of is what is going to take over the world tomorrow; not the tool or the good things we do with the tool. Froggie's problem is that he had listened to himself for so long that he couldn't hear what others were saying.

Well, dear folks, this also brings up the subject of prayer. There is a God who wants desperately to talk to us. He is willing to listen as long as we will let him talk ever so often. Now by talking, I mean that while he is talking, we are listening to what he has to say. If everything above is true and you know it is, then be rest assured we will have a hard time listening to a God whom we can't see and one who can't or doesn't text or e-mail or go to Facebook. We can't talk long if we do talk to God, because our attention span is so short.

Now if communications is the mode that builds relationships, this causes many problems in today's age. The personal touch of a relationship is taken away. Our minds are like Froggie's mind. We think about dreams and live in a fantasy world that is in the future, and it never comes to pass. We fail to communicate to others about the real world and today's subjects.

You see, folks, God so loved the world...he communicated to that world with hands on. He so loved that world that he sent his Holy Spirit to communicate the words of truth by talking to us... Yes, talking to us. Yes, by talking to us not because of something that we read or what someone else said but by talking to our heart so that we can know that it is him talking and that we can understand the words that he is saying to us. You see, that's the whole of it. The heart is the issue, and the computer will never communicate to the heart except to make it gravitate toward darkness. On the other hand, God will communicate to us and cause us to gravitate toward the light and the relationship that is very personal. There now you have it. Many like the impersonal of the technological age because they don't want to be exposed to that very revealing personal relationship with an all-knowing God. You can get away with stuff on the computer and hope they never find out. But if you talk to God and let him talk to you, you will know that he knows…and you can't hide any longer. In short, I asked a man at the altar if he wanted me to pray about what he had brought up or whether I should pray and let God speak through me. He stated quickly that I should just pray about what he had brought up and not anything else. He was afraid of what God might reveal.

So do you want to become personal and lay your computer aside when habit says not to? Do you want to enter into the presence of God and wait for him to talk? It will take time and a change of patterns, but it can be done. Your life may well be at stake at this time of your existence. I just know that if you will take as much time with God as you do with your computer, the spell that the evil one has laid on you will be broken. *As much time as…think less about your computer, and spend more time thinking about God.*

Do you know our bodies follow, for the most part, what we are thinking about? My wife had bought me a bicycle for Christmas. I hadn't ridden it much but decided to start because of gas prices and the need for exercise. I hadn't forgotten how to ride, but I did forget that for an older man, it wouldn't be like wearing a glove or something like that. I had to pay attention to every detail and look ahead at the pathway as to where I was going. I've almost rode into a ditch. I ran into the awing arm of our camper and almost ran into the house all because I wasn't paying attention to what I was doing.

In Hebrews, there are several places where the writer stresses the fact that we are to fix our eyes on Jesus, the author and perfecter of our faith (Heb. 12:2). Froggie was not the gift to the frog kingdom by going to the institute, nor are we the gift to mankind because of what we can accomplish. If we don't keep focused on who the Savior is, we will run amuck and slowly boil to death. You see, he is the only one that knows the ins and the outs of the life we are living. He is the only one who knows the past and what we had to go through to get to this point. He was there whether or not we were Christians, and he saw the skinned knee and the broken heart. He has this ability to know what needs healed if only we would stay focused.

God also knows where we are today. I know that you think that you see him walking with you every day, but you don't know the half of it. If he is the one to count the very hairs on our head, you have to believe that he sees our thoughts and desires and feelings all day long. He knows why we turn red when embarrassed or why we get frustrated when things don't go right, and he knows why fear takes over when there doesn't seem to be anything that is threatening us. He knows what the devil is up to, and he knows why the devil seems to have the ability to wreak havoc in our lives.

The God I serve has the ability to know the future. He's not just another physic that predicts things that he thinks are going to happen. He is the God of all time, and for some unknown reason, he knows all about all times. He knows where we are going next week, and he knows when we will get there. Nothing takes him by surprise, ever. He knows who we are going to meet, and he knows what they will means to us on that very day. He knows who will be president for the next term, and he knows who will give their hearts to Jesus. He even knows who will be the last one to get saved. Now listen, I had an evangelist tell me that God couldn't know that, because we have a free will. If we say he is all-knowing, it's just a matter of believing that it is true. Otherwise, let's not play the game and say he is all-knowing if we really believe that there are things that he doesn't know.

If he is the one that has all the details to our life within his mind, wouldn't it be good if we would stay focused on him? We can't trick him, the devil can't trick him, and other people can't trick him, end of sentence. He knows the way through the wilderness, and all we have to do is follow, by faith that is.

On the other hand, the computer knows so much more about us than we would like to admit. New technology is putting into place

84

things that would scare us to death if known. But it doesn't know our hearts. It doesn't know our future, and it doesn't know our will. The computer can only "predict" what our next step will be and what our next decision will be. The computer doesn't know what getting saved even means. Yes, the devil does, but he can only guess about the details that are involved. He does know that if we get into the hands of Jesus and we stay focused, we will make it home without losing our lives.

Some of you will have to adjust your focus, and it may be a difficult thing to do. You have focused on the newest program or game. You have focused on who you have to talk to and what you can buy next. You're on the computer so much that you don't have time or desire to focus on God or his Son. It will be a strain to let go of some of the things you have become so ingrained in. The "net" won't break so easily, and the "web" is so sticky that it will take a long time to get cleaned up. But, friend, it can be done. God is able to break you free before it is too late.

Today's people think so much of the advancement of technology and what the computer can do for us that we forget that the one who designed everything that is, is the one who sent his Son. We forget that before we discovered the atom God had already created it. When we reached into the depths of the sea, God had already created it. When we went to the outreaches of space, God had already created it. When we ask the computer what could be wrong with our loved one, God already knows and doesn't have several possibilities. When we match DNA and try to find a killer, God already knows who did it.

If we were half as amazed about who God is and what he can do as we are about what the computer can do, we would be miles ahead of where we are today. This, in turn, would allow us to study the God of the universe with new interest instead of studying old rhetoric of what we know about God. The old rhetoric is so important because it points us toward the Savior and who God is. But, folks, we have been studying that for years, and the vision gets dimmer as time goes on, and we treat God as if he were just another Bible story. I know, I know, you will tell me that it isn't so. We do claim that God is who he says he is. Then why on earth do we spend hours and hours in meetings telling how bad the economy is? We say, "He owns the cattle on a thousand hills and the wealth in every mine." But reality says that we treat him if he were broke. We have a form of lip service, but our hearts are far from him.

I guess that is the problem. We believe stuff about God, but rarely is it from our heart that we believe. We study to show ourselves approved and turn around and forget what we studied. When you focus on God, the only thing that will stick is what is captured by the heart, the center of our being. The mind then needs to be transformed so the body will act like it really believes. In other words, I enter into the ministry and preach all day long about the love of Jesus because I know that he saved me. It is a different story when something traumatic happens to a family member and I have to ask myself, "Does God really love me?"

Again, when I lose my job and the bills pile up, can God really provide all my needs according to his riches in glory? And what about when I am so tired that it doesn't seem like I can go on and he tells me I can do all things through Christ which strengthens me?

There is heart knowledge, and there is head knowledge. The computer will only give head knowledge; only God can give heart knowledge. Turn off the computer, and sit down with God, and ask him to talk to you. It may take some time to quiet your heart so that your ears can be open, to be still and know that he is God. Now if you can accomplish that one day, do it the next day. Make a habit and a pattern to follow every day. You won't be sorry you did. You will be happy forever if you do. Study God today. Don't just study about him. Trust me, he won't mind.

Prayer

Have you ever caught yourself muttering at your computer? It won't let you do a certain thing, and you are as frustrated as can be. More than that, have you realized that you talked to your computer and urged it to new heights and you really haven't said any "words" to it? Your mind has been very involved with what you want it to do, so much so that someone can come into the room and you don't hear them enter or you can't hear them when they talk to you? Sure you have. Quit pretending you haven't. I'm going to talk to you about prayer, a subject I know so little about because of the dynamics of why it works.

On one hand, you have a machine that can't turn itself on or off without being programmed to, and on the other hand, you have a God whom you can't see or (most of the time) can't hear. The machine can be programmed to anticipate what you might mean as you program in your desires. God knows before you even ask of him what your desires are. The machine can give you answers... Take spellcheck for instance. I am the world's worst speller. Whenever I make a mistake, the computer kicks in and tells me that I goofed again. It then gives me some choices to select from. But sometimes it tells me, "No spelling suggestions." It has no clue what I'm trying to say. God, on the other hand, not only knows what I'm trying to spell, but he also knows what I'm trying to say. I depend on the machine to correct my spelling, but as to the content of what I'm trying to say, I need God's help every time.

To pray "properly," one would have to believe in the one that you are praying to. *Is God really* there, and is he listening? *Can he* do anything with what I am telling him? *Does he care* enough to do anything with what I am telling him? *Is he going to* do anything with what I am telling him?

Secondly, if I am to pray properly, I will have to change my mind. I should not just look at prayer as a means of receiving answers to problems and questions that I have. I must remember that the whole of our salvation is to establish a relationship with God so we might have fellowship together with him. That relationship will include praise and adoration as well as conversation—conversation, not just questions and answers. God wants to talk with us like the bride that we are so love is developed in the heart as well as the head.

Thirdly, prayer must move from being a habit that I carry out religiously to the place where it becomes a need and a natural response to a loving heavenly Father. My granddaughter runs into my arms when I show up at the house. We play dolls, we go to the playground, we cook together, and every once in a while, I teach her things, "Don't do that," etc. But for the most part, we just enjoy each other. I'm not a threat to her in any way, and I don't condemn her, because I love her. If ever we would get past the law and become saved by the "Spirit of Christ," we wouldn't be condemned by God, and we would run into his arms daily. We wouldn't just have questions to be answered and problems to be solved. We would desire to be with the one who loves us most.

As we enter into the *holy place* where we meet with God, we find a peace that can't be compared with anything in the whole world. It takes a while to come to the realization that I have nothing to bring to the table that God needs. My knowledge, my strength, my ability are all wasted commodities when considered with the one that I am face to face with. What baffles my mind is why a God who is…so… much more than anything I could fathom would want to talk with me. I can see him wanting to answer my questions, the pitiful ignorant man that I am. I can see him wanting to fix all my problems, being the weakling that I am. I can see him wanting to provide for all my needs because he pities my inability to provide for myself. But, folks, for the life of me, I can't imagine why he would want to have conversations with me like we were friends. Maybe you can fathom that bit of insanity, but I cannot. You just don't realize what I've done or what I've thought. You don't realize how insignificant I really am. Or…maybe you think so highly of yourself that you think you deserve to be talked to by the sovereign God of Creation. Nevertheless, John tells us that we will know his voice when he speaks to us. Let's us enter in.

Get the relationship right, and the asking falls in line. You begin to find out what the Father would like, and your heart is now involved so his decision is okay with you.

Prayer

Help, I'm dying!
It's okay. Even if I let you die, you will live.
But I'm scared to death!

There is no fear in perfect love. Trust me
that I have it under control.
Are you sure?
Of course I'm sure. I wrote the book. All
I'm asking you to do is believe.

His Word

God is not a man, that He should lie,
nor the son of man, that he should change his mind.
Does he speak and then not act?
Does he promise and not fulfill? (Num. 23:19)

Have you heard all the promises about faster service, less expensive, broader coverage, and with more technological advancement? Our TV got burned in a lightning storm; but when we watched TV, before that, they were trying to sell you everything they could so you would buy they latest item. No matter what the promise was, it seemed that the promise became obsolete with the next promise. It also seemed to imply that because you were a genius, you could keep up with all the advancement. Not many of us are geniuses; so much of what we received was wasted. They couldn't make good their promises, because it depended on our genius mind. The other thing that I observed was how everything that they promised had a price tag attached to it. The cost seemed low enough if you didn't anticipate that you would have to pay more later or buy something new when this became old and outdated.

I don't know if you have looked into God's Word lately, and if you did, I don't know if you ran across any promises. If read correctly, you will find that from the get-go the Bible is full of the promise for you and me so that we can make it home to live forever with God. It has taken thousands of years to get us to the point we are at today, but we are at the door. His Word has been stretched in every way possible and in every situation possible and has been proven to be unchanging. The Word itself has been scrutinized to prove that it was just a set of rules and those rules were faulty. In every way, the twisting of time has tried to prove that God didn't care about you and me. But listen, friend, I have had the privilege to prove his Word true. Everything that could go wrong went wrong. Everything that could be needed was provided. In every way, God's Word has been tested in my life, and he has never failed at keeping his promises that connect me with the outcome of my life to get me home—unlike Froggie, who boiled for no reason except to become an experiment in some laboratory, who was boiled so man could claim some great advancement, so we could say in our pride, "Look what we have done."

Mankind will fail us, and so will the computer. Both are trying to lead us down a pathway of destruction. Slowly and surely it is taking place. But God and his Word will never fail those who trust him with all their heart. His Word came in the form of Jesus Christ. Yes, we will slowly be boiled to death as it says in Daniel, but the end is yet to come—the end as we see it but the beginning as God sees it. Trust his Word. Don't trust what man has made. Don't trust in the created things of this earth. Ask him to reveal where the lie has entered in, and he will tell you.

Poor Froggie, If He Had Only Listened.

A man was walking along a beach, and every now and then, he would pick up a starfish and throw it back into the ocean. Now there were many starfish on the beach, more than could possibly be thrown back in. Seeing his efforts, someone asked him why he was working at something that made such little difference to all those starfish. His answer was, "It made a difference to the one that I just threw back into the sea."

Some will say, "Why have you written such a book knowing that so many will reject the thought that our precious computer would happen to be the great delusion in 2 Thessalonians 2:11?" Obedience. At first, I thought different thoughts about the computer and didn't really believe that what I was saying was true. Now? I'm not so sure that what I have written isn't exactly true. It's not a point that I plan on arguing with anyone soon. Why? Because if you just take the warning that there is a plan that is out to get you and we are in the throes of the last days and that it is gradually sucking the life out of our Christianity, I will have perhaps saved one little starfish. I don't have to prove that I'm right. I do have to be obedient. This little book isn't going to win any prizes. But it will have saved my soul. I have warned those who will read and take heed. The rest? Maybe someone with more clout will come along and water the seed that I have planted. I love you, and so does the God of the universe. I've left out many, many stories about how I have been affected by what I have written because the book isn't about me.

Actually, the story is about a frog that went to a laboratory and the test was run to see how he would react to hot water. He did jump out when introduced to hot water but was boiled to death when introduced to cool water that was heated gradually until boiling hot. It remains that his life won't be in vain if we would receive his warning to us.

I believe with all my heart that the computer represents the tree of the knowledge of good and evil. You can eat both fruits from the tree. I have too many friends who have fallen because of partaking of the wrong fruit.

I believe that the pride of life is why many will not listen. They are ingrained with worshipping the created things instead of the creator. They want their little piece of the pie no matter how small it is.

I believe I will be labeled because of my old and antiquated ways of viewing life. But if you have read my book *From Chaos to Control*, you will know that God has done so much for me that I could care less what label people put on me.

I believe that in the coming days, we will see many things happen that will blow our minds. People will get elected and laws will be put in place because the people of this world have been hypnotized by a tool that is part of a plan to take over the world and discredit the God who created it and died for the people who live on it.

I believe that one day soon I will go to be with that Jesus who died for me so that I could live…forever.

Friend, what do you believe? Are you willing to stake your life on what you believe? Someday, you will have to make that choice.

The game of church will come to a close, and you will have to make that choice. What do you believe? Do you live what you say you believe, or are you like our computer friend who has to change with the sifting sand to the newest gadget and the latest fad?

God is old, friend, but I guarantee that he is not outdated. Try following him...with all your heart...with all your mind...with all your...

EPILOGUE

Froggie thought he had heard a noise some-where in the background of his mind. He was terrified to open his eyes, his body had poured a gallon of sweat, and he felt like he was in a burning pit.

Just how glad could one little bitty frog be when he did open his eyes!

He had been dreaming, and it seemed more like a nightmare. Papa frog had sent him to bed early because he hadn't listened to him about venturing to far from the pond. Froggie had always been sort of independent even when it came to obedience. He had always felt that he knew just a little more than everyone else. He had goals that went father than the other frogs, and daily he had set out to achieve them. Not anymore. If he was granted one more breath, he would tell his poppa and momma how sorry he was for not listening. He would apologize to his brothers and sisters for calling them stupid and slow and dull. He would apologize to King Frog for calling him antiquated in the way he had run the pond. He was sure now that the King knew way more than he did and that his personal plans would only get him in trouble down the road.

Froggie knew that he had to apologize to his friends because of how he had bragged to them about how superior he was. He would tell them how wrong he was concerning the ole pond that they lived in, that maybe they should be thankful for what they had instead of thinking of what he could have…out there!

Maybe Froggie would apologize to God if he existed for trying to build a tower of accomplishment to the heavens. Maybe he would apologize to God for trying to eat from two different worlds with two different types of fruit.

This I do know. Froggie was thrilled it had just been a dream.

ABOUT THE AUTHOR

Sharing the Gospel of Jesus Christ and the message for forty years seems fresher than ever. Boomer, as named by many; has preached to kids, teens, young adults, and even the old folks. He's pastored churches, held revivals and struck out with no plan, and witnessed to those God has led him to. His heart's desire is to prepare people for their final destination. Most recently, he has pastored at a drug and alcohol rehab center. Amazingly enough, the sparks have kindled a fire in his own heart as he preaches, teaches, and counsels men who are a half step away from eternity. He has considered most of these men as some of the best friends he ever encountered. Why? Because many have become his brother. When he gets home after staying for four days, he gets to tell his wife and kids and his small church that he pastors just what God has done. What a privilege that God has given him.

CPSIA information can be obtained
at www.ICGtesting.com
Printed in the USA
BVHW031203210321
603126BV00010B/455